Advance Praise

Inspiring and practical, this is the business-building system I used to grow my business. It's heart-centered and combines inner mindset work with practical strategies to create a 6-figure business. Chris takes the pressure and pushiness out of selling, offering a proven process that aligns perfectly for holistic coaches who value authenticity and want to grow their businesses without aggressive tactics.

Christina Nylese

Holistic Health and Recovery Coach

Underearning, financial struggle and burnout amongst wellness entrepreneurs, healers and coaches has been epidemic. Until Now. In this inspiring, easy to implement book, Williams gives you the playbook that can change everything.

If you follow her guidance, you will be successful and you will prosper.

Sara Connell bestselling author of The Science of Getting Rich for Women & Founder of Thought Leader Academy

The Soulful Abundance® System has been a total game changer not only for my business but for my life! I've dialed in so many amazing mindset and habit strategies that I never had before. I've learned how to think like an entrepreneur. I've worked on my own money mindset and things that could block my success. I've learned how to have systems and habits in place to grow my business. I know this intensive program has changed my life. If you're someone who is trying to grow a business and feel stuck or don't even know where to begin, this book is for you!

Jennifer Smith

Licensed Therapist and Certified Menopause Coach.

The Soulful Abundance System®

A 6-Step Guide to Building a Prosperous Six-Figure Holistic Business with Purpose

By
Christine Williams

Image Credits:

The majority of images in this book were created by the author. Two images were sourced from external rights holders and are used with permission. All images are either original or properly credited, and may not be reproduced without authorization.

The Thought Model on page 38 is used with permission from Brooke Castillo of The Life Coach School. All rights reserved.

Every effort has been made to trace the ownership of the image used in this publication. The image on page 160 of the statistics from Facebook and YouTube from the Pew Research Center which was sourced a publicly available online archive and is believed to be in the public domain or used under fair use for educational or informational purposes. No affiliation with or endorsement by the original creator, copyright holder, or associated foundation is implied. If there is a rights holder who believes this image has been used in error, please contact the publisher at operation@museliterary.com to request appropriate credit or removal.

Printed in the United States of America

Hardcover ISBN: 978-1-967703-05-0

Paperback ISBN: 978-1-967703-04-3

Library of Congress Control Number: Applied for

Muse Literary Publishing

Send feedback to hello@museliterary.com

Special discounts for bulk sales are available, please contact operations@museliterary.com

TABLE OF CONTENT

CHAPTER 1..1

PART 1 THE SOULFUL ABUNDANCE SYSTEM®........... 23

CHAPTER 2 ALIGNMENT CREATES ABUNDANCE...... 25

CHAPTER 3... 41

CHAPTER 4 STEP 2 DESIGN 73

CHAPTER 5... 119

CHAPTER 6 STEP THREE:ATTRACT............................. 127

CHAPTER 7 STEP 4:NURTURE.................................... 145

CHAPTER 8 STEP 5-INVITE...................................... 171

CHAPTER 9 STEP SIX:EMPOWER 193

PART 2 THE SHORT-TERM STRATEGY TO MAKING MONEY IN YOUR BUSINESS. 217

PART 3 SOULFUL ABUNDANCE STORIES 231

AN INVITATION TO YOU 255

ACKNOWLEDGMENTS 257

ENDNOTES AND RESOURCES............................. 261

FAVORITE BOOKS.. 263

YOUTUBE VIDEOS/ CHANNELS 265

PODCASTS.. 267

ABOUT THE AUTHOR... 269

Chapter 1

"The future belongs to those who believe in the beauty of their dreams." — **Eleanor Roosevelt.**
"She Believed She Could, So She Did"- **unknown.**

From Stay-at-Home Mom to 7-Figure Business Owner

I was stranded at a gas station in South Carolina with my three boys and did not have enough gas to get home to North Carolina. I put my credit card into the gas pump slot and saw the message: DECLINED. I started to sweat. Thoughts began to race through my mind. I told myself, *Just try it again. The machine is probably broken or glitching.* I wiped the card on my shorts and tried again. DECLINED... again. I started to feel dizzy. My heart was beating fast. I was 200 miles away from home and had three kids depending on me.

While I was trying to figure out how I would get home, my youngest son popped into the front seat of the minivan and asked if he could get some pretzels for a snack. Absentmindedly, in the way all moms do, I told him, "Not today, honey. We have snacks that I brought with us." I fumbled in my purse to see if I had another card I could use. I grabbed my debit card and swiped it. DECLINED. I tried to be calm for my boys, but inside, I was starting to panic. I slowed down my breath and tried to think of some options. Okay, Chris, I said to myself.

There is always a way. Just stay calm so the kids stay calm, and THINK.

This was the first time since I was a kid that I felt the panic of having no resources to my name. I was hours away from home, in the middle of nowhere, and the weight of this responsibility—along with the sense of shame that I had put my kids in danger—almost sent me into an anxiety attack. It was a pivotal moment, and I vowed I would NEVER be in this position again.

My mind raced through options of how I could get the money to buy enough gas to get home. Maybe I could wash some dishes in the restaurant part of the gas station to make enough money? What would I do with the boys if I had to do that? Did I have anything in the car I could sell? I thought of those people you see on the side of the road holding up signs asking for bus fare to get home—or the homeless parents asking for money to feed their children. I asked myself, How the hell did this happen? How did I get here?

I'd lived a very normal and comfortable life on a 50-acre farm in a sweet town in North Carolina. I'd never been in a position before where there wasn't some sort of resource I could pull from if we needed something. I thought about who I could call. We were on our way home from visiting my mom, so I called her to see if she could help. Thankfully, she was able to wire some money into my bank account quickly so I could fill up the gas tank and get home. But what a lesson in humility it was—having to ask for help and rely on the generosity of someone else to change the situation.

I felt shame and guilt. Memories came rushing in from when I was a kid, and we were on food stamps. The fear of not enough felt like a daily occurrence. I remembered making mayonnaise sandwiches and hiding the Doritos from my brother so he wouldn't eat them all.

That day at the gas station, I decided I would never be in this position again. I doubly vowed that I would become financially independent. I would create what I needed and make sure I was in an empowered state, able to make my own choices instead of being dependent upon someone else.

I had been a stay-at-home mom for the past 17 years, raising my boys. I never thought I even needed to put aside money for myself. Everything I did was for my kids and the family. I homeschooled my boys, we had an organic garden, and I taught part-time yoga classes to contribute what little I could to our expenses. I had all my basic, primary needs taken care of. My emotional needs were another story.

My ex-husband and I were caught in a toxic emotional pattern that was killing both of us. So when it came time to call it quits after 17 years, I was starting over in my life in my late 40s with nothing but some child support, alimony, and the determination to create happiness and stability for myself and my boys.

I was determined to create my own wealth and financial security somehow. I wanted choices. Freedom. A rich and abundant life in all its forms. The word rich is about more than just money for me. It's about having the resources not only for myself but also to have an overflow so I can share with others. It's providing for my family, contributing to my boys' education, donating to the local food bank, having time to travel and share the cultures of the world with my kids, and providing experiences for others.

I didn't want to make money just for the sake of making money. I wanted to create a life of wealth that would expand my joy, fulfillment, and contribution to the world. I wanted to help other women do the same—women just like me who wanted to impact the world with their gifts and be cheered on as they created wealth, abundance, joy, and love in their lives on their own. And FREEDOM.

I wanted to create freedom for myself, my kids, and other women. Freedom to make choices that align with their values, passions, missions, and desires. Freedom to smash through the glass ceilings that have held women back. Freedom to leave unhealthy circumstances if they needed to. And freedom to be empowered business owners, sharing services that make our world a better place.

My passion for supporting women came from my grandmother, Paula. As a child, she would take me with her to the Equal Rights Amendment marches in Washington, D.C., to stand up for women's rights. It was important to her that I grew up in a world where women could be anything they wanted to be—to have the same rights, the same freedoms, and the same pay as men.

I watched and saw the power of community as women gathered together on the mall and marched, chanting, "1-2-3-4, we need three more," all the way to the Capitol. The energy of thousands of women linking arms, standing up for something important to them, and not being afraid to be seen or use their voices was electrifying. I joined in with my voice, too, and felt part of something so much bigger than myself—a movement that was powerful and important.

I had no idea how these early years would impact my life—how they would lead me to create communities of women and help them move beyond the limitations and cultural entrainments we grew up with.

As I look back on the courage I had to find within myself and the obstacles I had to overcome, I hear my grandmother's voice loud and clear: Chris, you can do anything you want. You are strong, you are beautiful, you are powerful, and I will cheer you on all the way.

Even though she grew up in a time when women couldn't own property, hold a credit card, or even vote, they did not stay quiet. My great-grandmother, Ella, marched in the first women's suffrage march in Washington, D.C., with her mother. They used their voices. They were told no, and they didn't listen. They kept fighting for what was important to them, their daughters, and future generations.

I am beyond grateful to have the freedoms I do today because of them.

Supporting women is in my bloodline. I witnessed the resilience of women firsthand. I saw how they overcame limitations. I knew I could do it, too.

I didn't know how yet, and I was scared, but I had this fire in me to figure it out—to step into my power and create the life I wanted, not the life someone else said was possible or acceptable.

When I got back home from the road trip to see my mom, I started to plan my next steps. I decided that I would go to massage school so I could have some way to take care of myself and the boys. It was a yearlong certification, and I could still homeschool the boys and keep some sense of normalcy for them while I completed the process. I could complete my certification and learn what I needed to learn to open my own business and build some financial independence. This was a way for me to continue to be a present mama to my boys and follow my heart for natural health, wellness, and healing.

I had wanted to get a massage therapy certification many years earlier when I was a stay-at-home mom and was told no by my husband. Now that I was on my own, I was ready to jump on this opportunity. I negotiated in our separation agreement that he would pay for my training since I needed a way to support myself and my children. I have always had a love for wellness and helping others with their well-being. I became interested in holistic health and began researching it when I was a teen. So when I began envisioning the ways that I could support myself and my boys, a holistic path was a natural one. I saw it as a way to follow my heart for serving others, helping them live happier, healthier lives, opening my own business, creating a livelihood that would support my family, and still being able to make my own schedule and be available for my boys and their activities.

I had no idea what was involved in opening a business, but I knew I would figure it out. So, with the divorce agreement that my ex-husband and I agreed upon, I started my schooling and my journey as a female small business owner.

These life-changing events happened in 2012, and that original intuitive pull to follow my heart put me on the path to growing a thriving seven-figure business and helping other women do the same. Since then, I've paid off all my credit card debt, paid off my car, paid for two kids to go through college without loans, bought a car and a house in my own name, and taken my family on amazing trips to make memories.

Together, we have been able to experience the joys of life and the cultures of the world. We've gone to Iceland and Italy and traveled to different states in the U.S. to explore mountains, hike, enjoy nature, and be together. Just this past summer, I checked off a big bucket list item—I got to visit the lavender fields in Provence, France. I took three weeks to hike the Alps, take my family to Paris, visit Catalonia, and enjoy making memories.

For the first time in my life, I was able to buy a new car without needing a father or husband to co-sign for me. I went from being a divorced stay-at-home mom of 17 years who was $30,000 in debt with no room on my credit cards, no job, and only a dream to crossing the $1,000,000 mark in my business. That is a long way from being stranded at a gas station with just $25 in my bank account. If I can do it, you can too.

Today, I am the CEO of Shine Wellness LLC and the founder of Activate Abundance® Academy, a business accelerator program for women wellness coaches and holistic practitioners. It's a woman-owned and woman-run company supporting female health and wellness coaches and holistic practitioners to create thriving six-figure and beyond businesses without trading their well-being or integrity for success.

I've been featured on the cover of Women Thrive magazine, in PREEMINENCE MAGAZINE, NBC, CBS, Forbes Coaches Council, ABC, FOX, USA Today, Google News, Digital Journal, and more. I am a sought-after speaker who has helped hundreds of women just like you pursue their dream of going into business for themselves. I have helped countless more build profitable and sustainable businesses using my Soulful Abundance System®. The pathway and framework of the Soulful Abundance System® easily guide others simply and soulfully to achieve their dreams.

With over 30 years of experience as a wellness practitioner, I know how it goes. I have the training, certifications, and letters after my name: Certified Yoga Teacher, Master Holy Yoga

Teacher, Licensed Massage and Bodywork Therapist, Certified Functional Nutritional Therapy Practitioner, Certified Health and Life Coach, Certified Mastery Transformational Coach, Certified Money Breakthrough Business Coach, Certified Sacred Money Archetypes Coach, Certified True Intuition Coach, and Certified Soulful Business and Leadership Coach. As you can see, I have been multi-passionate in many modalities along my entrepreneurial journey.

In this book, I can't wait to share with you what I have learned on my journey and give you the tools to do the same if you choose. I know what it's like to start from scratch—to rebuild your life and reinvent yourself to match what you truly love to do without funding or loans. And I want you to know this is possible for you, too.

Recently, I came across a statistic that had me shaking my head and made me even more determined to support women in building thriving and sustainable businesses that allow them to be well-paid, do what they love, and have a life of freedom.

According to Women Entrepreneurs[1], 88% of women entrepreneurs make below $100,000. And 90% of wellness coaches never cross the Six-Figure line.

I couldn't believe that statistic. Why were women in the holistic wellness profession struggling so much to create a decent wage? And if they were struggling, that meant they were not

---

[1] https://writersblocklive.com/blog/women-entrepreneurs-statistics/

serving the people who most needed their help. The people who were sick and suffering were still in their pain.

What I saw was a lot of women who had a desire to make an income, share their gifts, and make an impact on the world with no practical instruction on how to do that. What they had was an expensive hobby, not a thriving business. They had gotten the certifications and training to help others but had no understanding of how to actually start and build a profitable business. I saw they were just like me when I started—filled with big dreams and desires but lacking the practical steps and trusted mentorship to collapse the timeline to their success.

The problem when you are first starting out is that you don't know what you don't know. There are specific foundations that need to be in place. These can range from the simplest things, like how to take payment or set up a scheduling system, to time-blocking so you can work in and on your business without burning out. You may not understand how to market yourself effectively and authentically or where to find paying clients so you can actually bring cash flow into your business. There is a LOT to learn.

So why aren't these schools setting up their students for success? Because that's not what they are there to do. Their job is to teach a skill or a modality—like health coaching, nutritional therapy, energy work, healing touch, sound therapy, life coaching, or massage therapy. Their certification programs are not set up to teach the basics of marketing and sales. And yet, that is what is required to have a profitable and sustainable business today.

Students are being told, "If you build it, they will come." I can't tell you how many of my clients come to me feeling disheartened because their schools and training programs told them to just rely on word of mouth and they would have a thriving business. That is just not true. That is not how businesses grow and become successful.

I have made it my mission to turn this statistic upside down. When my business started thriving, colleagues asked me what I was doing. I began to share how I built my health coaching and nutritional therapy practice. This happened so often that I decided to reverse-engineer exactly what I did so I could share my process with more women in a structure that would be repeatable. I wanted to create a system that would not only teach the basics but give a proven pathway on what to focus on and at the right time.

No more just throwing spaghetti at the wall to see what sticks or chasing tactics that feel out of alignment with the way they want to grow a business. This system has proven to accelerate business growth and collapse the timeline to success.

In my journey, I have noticed this weird cultural entrainment that we, as women, have taken on that prevents us from asking for help—like we should know it all already, and asking for help is a weakness. This leads many women to try to do this all on their own. They piece together the information they see others using and try to lone-wolf it.

This lone-wolf mentality is one of the most harmful aspects of being a solopreneur. We are not meant to do this work alone, sweet friend. Women thrive in a community. Humans are pack animals. There is an internal drive to be a part of a tribe. If you think back to our ancestors, being kicked out of a tribe meant you died. Community meant safety, belonging, and life.

And yet, today, we have this crazy idea that we should figure things out on our own. There is this superwoman mentality I see women take on that makes it hard for them to ask for help—a false belief we have picked up that you need to do ALL the things and do them well.

Keep juggling all those balls—mom life, wife, friend, caregiver, money maker, business owner—and oh, by the way, make sure to smile, be friendly, never complain, ask for help, or let them see you struggle.

GAHHHH! It's just not real life, my friend.

The first year I was in business as a functional nutritional therapy practitioner, I made a whopping $1,000. I didn't know what I didn't know. I had no guidance on what to focus on and how to set up the systems that make a six-figure business not only possible but scalable and joyful.

So, I decided to ask for help. I had been following a business coach online for a couple of years and really liked the way she was growing her business. She was generous with her knowledge, cultivated a community of other women, and was inspiring to listen to and watch.

I booked a call with her, and right away, I joined a year-long coaching program. I knew I needed the support, and yet I had no idea how I was going to pay her. It was a $10,000 investment, and I was barely making ends meet. I only had $100 in my checking account to pay her a deposit. I was short by hundreds of dollars for even the first month's payment.

But I KNEW I needed help to get me where I wanted to go quickly. Success leaves clues, so I looked around at other successful six-figure coaches, and they ALL had a business coach. Not to mention, I felt really excited about having this particular coach support me so I could build my business in a way that felt aligned with being a heart-centered coach who served generously and made people her priority.

Saying yes to coaching with her was a pivotal moment for me. It showed me that I was stepping out of the scarcity mentality—allowing circumstances to determine my decisions—and seeing what a powerful creator I actually was, regardless of what my bank account said. She supported me in coming up with some ways to bring in cash quickly, and within that first month, I had created $1,000. By the end of month two, I had created $10,000, and in six months, I had created six figures. If I had let my bank account decide whether or not to get support, I would not be writing this book or have been able to help transform the lives of so many other women.

Christine Williams

Seeing a new possibility when faced with an obstacle or challenge can be a lot tougher when we're trying to figure out all the pieces on our own. It's impossible to read the label when we are inside the bottle.

But there is a way around this. Let me share what I do... and what I don't do.

I don't listen to that voice in my mind that says, "You can't figure this out." I know success leaves clues. And I also know that NO ONE builds a thriving "anything" on their own. So, again, I reached out and asked for help. Today, I have a team of people who support me. I've hired a mindset coach, a financial coach, and a strategy coach. I've invested in masterminds with other women entrepreneurs creating success. We cheer each other on and stretch each other to believe and take action on our dreams.

Being a part of these communities with a high level of mentorship—having someone who has walked the path before me—has been one of the biggest game changers in my business. Community. Women linking arms. Just like when I was a little girl marching on the Capitol with my grandmother. There is power in lifting each other up, learning, and growing together. We are not meant to do this work alone, and we don't need to.

If you're reading this, you've taken the first step. However, it happened that this book landed in your hands. It's no accident. I don't believe the universe works that way. I believe information comes to us at exactly the right time—when we need it most.

I believe you're here because you were born with a tremendous passion for serving others and have something wonderful to share with the world. As a health coach, wellness coach, or holistic practitioner, you went into this business to help others live and lead happier, healthier lives. And you deserve to be well-paid to share those gifts with others and have the freedom to work in a way that allows you to enjoy life.

For me, I love to travel with my family. Experiences with my loved ones are memory makers for me, and it's those connections and the time to live fully that I value.

I'm here to do everything I can to champion you to confidently create both wealth and well-being without trading your integrity for success. To move beyond just surviving and into thriving and overflowing—so you can have more than enough to share rather than just getting by or, worse, giving up.

I want you to see your dreams realized and to feel financially and personally empowered along your entrepreneurial journey. To be a role model for the next generation of women who desire to smash those glass ceilings and create the businesses and lives they love—to even become the breadwinners of the family. I've witnessed so many of my colleagues retiring their spouses and creating amazing relationships in the process.

No matter what stage of business you are in, I 100% believe you can build a profitable and sustainable business that you feel fulfilled doing while being in the flow and out of the hustle that so many impact-driven entrepreneurs can fall into.

When women create their own wealth, amazing things happen. They gain a seat at the table to make big decisions in their world and on a larger scale. It creates a ripple effect and transformation on multiple levels. Women creating financial wealth and freedom are role models for the next generation of what's possible. They have more choices in how they want to live and are empowered to use their wealth as a vehicle for making the world better.

I want you to not only see this as possible but to make it a reality. When you shine, it shows others it's possible, too. When women come together in a community with a vision, the impact that it creates is like compound interest—the benefits exponentially grow over time.

I want to share the story of my client Sally, who went from bankruptcy to six figures in one year. Before our work together, she had certifications as a health coach and had been through the expensive master's training that promised $10,000 months from her coaching school, but she was still struggling to get her business off the ground.

She had the passion. She had the tools to help her clients create transformation in their lives. But she didn't have the right business tools or systems to create those consistent $10,000 months.

She had been taught one method of "getting" clients, and it made her feel sales-y and not at all aligned with the way she wanted to build her business. She didn't want to use the outdated, aggressive marketing or slimy sales tactics we see out there today to make sales and have a profitable business. She wanted a heart-centered way of serving others and nurturing relationships so that it felt easy to invite clients to take the natural next step to work with her.

Like most of us, she was sick of trying to overcome objections, convince or persuade people to work with her or trade her well-being and integrity for success. She began to work with me and started using The Soulful Abundance System you will learn in these chapters, to design the life and business she wanted. BOTH—a family life, homeschooling her three kids, time and freedom to enjoy playing in the creek, and a thriving business that created financial freedom for her family.

By implementing these steps, she went from bankruptcy to over $100,000 in just one year. And countless others have done the same. They've stepped out of jobs they hated and situations that left them feeling disempowered. They have gotten out of poverty and have created lives and businesses they love— businesses that impact our world for the better.

Let's change the world together. Let's move out of the patriarchal and cultural entrainments that keep women playing small. Let's create new beliefs that show the world that women can be powerful and feminine. Smart and beautiful. Kind and successful. Generous and have clear boundaries.

They can be the breadwinners and income generators and have fulfilling marriages and relationships. So much is possible, and in sharing this book with you, it is my mission to help you achieve all of this.

Over the course of this book, I'll be sharing with you the same 6-step Soulful Abundance System® that I've used to grow my business to $1,000,000,000 in just three years. It's also what I teach my clients inside Activate Abundance® Academy. I'll keep it simple and focused, with real-life examples, so you can implement these game-changing principles, too. Plus, I'll be sure to share the often forgotten but so important keys to nurturing ourselves, our businesses, and our connections. I'll be weaving these throughout our journey, as we can't build sustainably or profitably without them.

I have mentioned The Soulful Abundance System® many times. What is The Soulful Abundance System®? It is a 6-step system to a heart-centered six-figure business and beyond. Below is a breakdown of what it looks like.

• **Step ONE:** ✿ **ALIGN** – Gain CLARITY on your soulful business, your soulmate client, and YOUR unique brilliance so you can feel confident in building the business that's right for you.

• **Step TWO:** ✿ **DESIGN** – CREATE a purpose-driven plan around two CORE main offers with a simple, Soul-Aligned Strategy.

• **Step THREE:** ✿ **ATTRACT** – MAGNETIZE your messaging to ATTRACT SOULMATE CLIENTS into your ecosystem and community, where they can feel connected and part of something special.

• **Step FOUR:** 🌸 **NURTURE** – CAPTURE their hearts and NURTURE the relationship with high-value training in exclusive masterclasses or workshops they love.

• **Step FIVE:** 🌸 **INVITE** – Give your soulmate clients the invitation to say YES to their transformation. Release all false beliefs and limitations and make the SOULFUL EXCHANGE. This is where a soulful sale happens.

• **Step SIX:** 🌸 **EMPOWER** – Your clients are seeking heartfelt empowerment, and YOU are the one to gift it to them. Reprogram the limitations of what you think you can achieve and uncover an exciting new sense of freedom that invites the ABUNDANCE you deserve. Stand up and be a LEADER. Develop yourself, inspire, and embolden others—because that's how it goes in a love-based paradigm.

In Step ONE, **ALIGN** – Alignment creates abundance. We'll dive into the importance of the inner game—mindset. Without the inner work done first, the strategy (outer game) won't be effective. This is where we claim, from the very beginning, our worthiness and value and stand in the truth that we are already six-figure business owners.

We will also uncover your unique brilliance, align with what most lights you up—not just what makes money—and determine who you are here to serve with your gifts. Alignment is the key to creating the impact and income you desire.

Step TWO is **DESIGN** for success. We will take a look at designing your best business model and profit plan so you can serve with soul and create the high-end programs and offers that your ideal clients crave. We will also cover the importance of creating your own signature system so you can be a stand-out leader in your field. In this step, we'll design your own sacred self-care plan to keep you fully sourced and joyful instead of heading down burnout alley.

Step THREE is **ATTRACT**. In Step 3, I will share the Nurture Method®, which is the cornerstone of your success. Now that you know who you serve, how you help them, and have a profit plan in place, it's time to attract your ready-yes clients—not the tire kickers or the freebie seekers, but the real people who are looking for the solution you have to share and are ready to invest in themselves to make the transformation.

Step FOUR is **NURTURE**. Once you attract and start creating a community, you want to nurture your clients and make people your priority. Giving value, being generous, and helping your potential clients create wins before they buy from you builds trust and a community of raving fans. I'll share with you how to cultivate those connections so that working with you is the natural next step.

Step FIVE is **INVITE** to enroll. Serving and giving value is amazing, but you won't have a business if you leave people hanging on pain island. You must actually invite people to work with you. And hear me on this—making sales in your business does NOT need to feel sales-y. As a matter of fact, if it feels sales-y for you, it's going to feel sales-y for your potential client, and that type of relationship will only backfire in the end. I'll share a simple and fun way to invite people to invest in themselves by joining you in your programs or offers so that they get what they most want.

Step SIX is **EMPOWER** to Mastery. Here is where we get to be masterful at our systems and processes. It's time to repeat, learn, gather feedback, and do it again. Instead of chasing another bright, shiny object or tactic, double down on what you've learned. Pivot and tweak where you need to, and stay the course. As an entrepreneur, you're in it for the long game. Building resilience and endurance to recalibrate and align is what allows you to scale to your next level.

You didn't pick up this book by accident, my friend. If you're reading this, it's because you want something better for yourself, your family, and your life. You desire financial freedom doing what you love and the time to enjoy your wealth. You want a simple, heart-centered, authentic, and profitable six-figure business without high-pressure sales tactics or sacrificing your health, sanity, or family in the process.

The best way to use this book is to read it chapter by chapter and in order. Each chapter provides a foundation that is essential to understand to build a thriving business. We don't run before we learn to walk, so let's make sure you are taking the right steps to achieve the success of your dreams.

By reading this book, my hope is that you know exactly what to do, that you're not alone, and that you deserve to be well-paid for sharing your gifts with others. Building a six-figure–and-beyond business that lights you up is not only possible, but it's also predictable when you implement these steps. Being financially empowered allows you greater choices to serve, give, and change the world in the ways that matter most to you.

Ready to do this together? Let's dive in.

Part 1
The Soulful Abundance System®

"Women belong in all places where decisions are being made. It shouldn't be that women are the exception." — **Ruth Bader Ginsburg.**

"The way to achieve your own success is to be willing to help somebody else get it first." — **Iyanla Vanzant.**

Your 6-step framework to activate financial abundance and a sustainable, holistic business. These six steps create the foundation you need to build a six-figure or seven-figure business. They are the basics I return to repeatedly in my own business and the businesses of my clients. I am so excited to share them with you.

Chapter 2
Alignment Creates Abundance

The Abundance Formula

Inner Game (Mindset + Energetic Alignment) + Outer Game
(Strategy + Inspired Action) = **ABUNDANCE**

The Abundance Formula to create a six-figure wellness
business is simple and has been proven to work time and time
again. If you follow the formula in the right order, abundance is
yours. No matter what you desire to create, starting with the
inner game is always the most important place to begin.

**Inner Game (Mindset + Energetic Alignment) + Outer
Game (Strategy + Inspired Action) = ABUNDANCE**

Your inner game, or mindset, determines the thoughts and
feelings that will either propel you in the direction of abundance
or into scarcity. And your mindset is always in play, even
unintentionally. You see, your brain is always on, and it's
thinking constantly. Unfortunately, most of these thoughts are
subconscious and have been playing on repeat for quite some
time. You've been thinking thoughts that create feelings of joy
and happiness or fear and scarcity, which then lead you to act,

not act, or even react. So, while we can say we want a six-figure practice, the beliefs we hold about ourselves and that possibility need to line up so the action we take is effective. The problem is that many of our beliefs were created when we were little, and they are not helpful in where we are today or where we want to go. The brain wants us to avoid pain, seek pleasure, and conserve energy, so we are in an unconscious thought loop that just keeps playing based on our experiences of the past. Those thoughts are creating the reality of what you are experiencing today.

For example, if you had a time in your young life when you spoke up and were criticized for your views, chances are that today, you carry around a fear of being judged and criticized. Your brain marked that as something to notice and protect you from in the future. Fast forward 30 years, and you want to share something powerful and let your voice be heard—yet that same old thought will be playing in the background, telling you not to do it. That you will be judged, criticized, and lose a sense of security and belonging. So even though you're not in that same situation today as when you were a kid, your brain is keeping you safe from experiencing that sense of embarrassment again. And it's all happening automatically.

Your beliefs about yourself and the world program what you see in the world. What you see and focus on then creates an experience, and that experience leads back to support that belief. So, if you're afraid of being judged, you'll be looking for evidence in the world that you are being judged and that it's not safe to share your opinion. You'll find all sorts of reasons and evidence to continue to support this.

Circumstance:

Something that happens in our world Thought:

The meaning we make about what happened Feeling:

How that thought and meaning make us feel Action:

How we act, react, or take no action in response to the feeling Result:

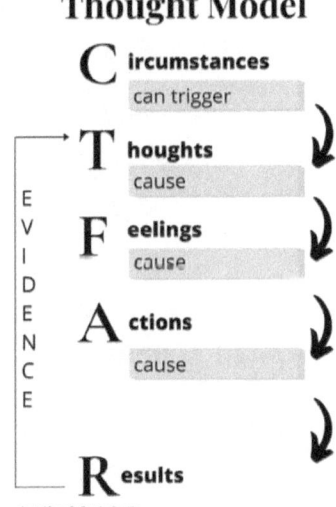

Thought Model

C ircumstances
can trigger

T houghts
cause

F eelings
cause

A ctions
cause

R esults

EVIDENCE

adapted from By Brooke Castillo

The result of our actions, which serves as evidence for our beliefs.

This Mindset Thought Model is a great feature to have if we need protection from something really dangerous, like a bear at our campsite, but it's not useful for taking action to grow our business and be visible to those we are most meant to help.

The good news is that our brains can be rewired. This is called neuroplasticity, and it's totally cool. You can use your conscious mind to change those old beliefs that no longer serve you so that you can think thoughts that FEEL amazing, take inspired action, get the results you desire, and begin to look for evidence in the world to support you even more in what's possible.

The key here is that whatever results you are experiencing in your life right now, they all stem from a previous thought. If you want to change your results, you must start by changing your thoughts.

Inner Game (Mindset + Energetic Alignment) + Outer Game (Strategy + Inspired Action) = ABUNDANCE

Aligning your thoughts to WHO you are in the world is the second part of the Inner Game and a critical component of the Abundance Formula. This is where you intentionally choose who you want to BE (an empowered six-figure coach or practitioner) and how that future version of you would think, FEEL, and act.

When I wanted to begin creating $10,000 months, I started each morning with the thought that this month was a $10,000 month. I thought this intentionally every day, and I started showing up in the world, thinking and acting from the place of it already happening. And guess what happened? You guessed it—I created a $10,000 month.

Now, I know that sounds really woo-woo but stay with me here. When I said, "This month is a $10,000 month," I stated it as if it were true. It was happening now—like I had just placed my order on Amazon and was awaiting delivery. I saw it in my imagination and felt like it was on its way. I felt confident, certain, and in joyful expectation. And because of that, I was energetically aligning with my desire, NOT with the lack of money in my bank account.

What you focus on grows. Therefore, I had to focus on my desire for what I wanted, not on what I lacked. Focusing on lack would only create more lack. Emotions are energy, and the emotion of lack is fear, doubt, and scarcity.

However, for me, the emotion of abundance and financial security is confidence, certainty, joy, freedom, and safety. Thinking thoughts that evoke those feelings energetically aligns me to see more of that in my world and attract more experiences that bring me wealth, security, freedom, confidence, certainty, and joy. Other thoughts that I use daily to create that feeling are, "Money loves me" and "Clients come to me easily."

You can grab a copy of my empowering money beliefs by going to the book portal here.

Here's one to get you started.

"I am positively expecting great results, no matter what I see in front of me. The universe is rearranging itself for my best interest right now."

The secret to feeling it and believing it is to really feel it in your body. Move beyond just the words and into the feeling of seeing it happening in the now. Even doing this for just two minutes a day can have a huge impact. Belief work is powerful, and you need to repeat this work multiple times a day. It's like building muscle or training for a race. You wouldn't just go to the gym once and think you were getting stronger. You would go repeatedly, day after day, to get stronger and stronger. The same happens when you want to rewire your thoughts. You are always thinking thoughts, so consciously choosing puts the power back in your hands instead of feeling like you are a victim of circumstances. I do this daily. It's called my daily alignment practice.

Don't skip this step. While it seems simple, it's actually 85% of your success.

My client, Marge, is an energy healer, but she was having trouble charging appropriate rates for her services. Even when some of her colleagues told her that her rates were too low and that she should raise them, her mind kept playing an old tape from long ago that said, "You can't be spiritual and charge money for your services. If you really wanted to help people, you would give your services away for free." She was trapped in what I call the "Starving Healer" mindset. She wanted to raise her rates, but she was being blocked by thoughts that were not serving her or the clients she was here to help.

The first thing we did was begin working on her money mindset. We created a belief plan for her so she could develop empowering beliefs about receiving money for her services and feel excited to see the changes her clients were making by working with her. She practiced this belief plan daily—on repeat and with emotion. Soon after we began, she raised her rates, and now she is not only attracting clients who are happy to pay her new rate, but she is also confidently owning the value of her wisdom and experience with over five decades as a healer.

According to Wayne Dyer, you can't feel bad enough to make someone else happy. I believe the same is true for wealth. You can't be poor enough to make someone else wealthy. Not charging for your services serves no one. It only keeps you in scarcity, lacking what you need, and limits the amount of energy and resources you need to really help others.

Christine Williams

When you got your coaching certificate or holistic practitioner certification, did you take a vow of poverty? How about a vow of silence?

Did you ask your school or program to give their program to you for free?

I bet you invested time, money, and energy in learning, practicing, and honing your skills. Now, as an expert in your field, you want to use it to help others AND be compensated in the process.

Remember this when:

- You are sharing your message.

- You set your pricing for your services appropriately (or raise them).

- You invite someone to step into their next level of transformation by working with you.

You are DESERVING of being compensated for your gifts.

You are DESERVING of sharing your voice and message so more people can get out of their struggle.

You staying quiet serves NO ONE. Giving away your services removes the opportunity for clients to invest their energy, which is essential for them to fully commit to their growth and achieve the transformation they desire. Never lose sight of that, even when doubt, fear, or other people's opinions kick in.

Women wellness entrepreneurs are here to change the world. Trust yourself. Know your self-worth and charge accordingly. Be visible so people can find you. There are people looking for the solution you provide NOW. Be brave. Be resilient. Your work matters, and it's safe for you to make a soulful exchange and share your voice. The more people you help, the more income you receive, and the more you can share.

So create a new belief plan to BE the empowered leader you are, and let's start changing our world.

Your Turn: Create Your Belief and Possibility Plan

When you are ready, grab a piece of paper and answer these questions. It's really important to WRITE these down and not just think about them. Writing uses a different part of the brain than just thinking. Studies show that when you write down your goals, you are 30% more likely to achieve them.

What do you desire?

Write it out in the present tense. Example: I create $10,000 months with ease.

- What does that look like, feel like, or sound like?

- Who are you with?

33

- How will you know you have it?

Use your imagination and as many descriptive words as you can.

Next, list 10 reasons why this outcome is possible and inevitable to achieve.

If you fully trusted yourself, what would you believe about YOURSELF to achieve this goal? Who do you need to BE in the world to achieve this goal? Example: confident, relaxed, certain, powerful, brave, determined, resourceful.

What is the future you—the one who already has what she desires—saying, feeling, thinking, and doing? What choices is she making? What might a normal day look like for her? Write it out as if it's already happening in the present. Use words like I AM... I have... I receive... I celebrate... I am so grateful for...

Read your belief plan every morning and every night for the next 30 days.

Even better—say it out loud. Speak as if it's actually happening and FEEL it.

Grab a friend and have them play along with you. We call this future pulling, and it's a powerful creation exercise. You can leave each other a message every morning starting with:

"I am so excited to share that... (I just had a new client reach out to me and wants to pay in full for my highest-priced offer.)"

or

"I'm so excited... (I just looked at my bank account, and I created my first $10,000 month! This feels amazing. This is the most I have ever created, and this is just the beginning. I'm so happy—I'm having a dance party in my kitchen!)"

There are many ways to do belief work, and lots of books and techniques out there beyond the scope of this book. I've shared what I do, and you can find more of my favorite resources here.

Here is another way I teach my clients to stay focused on what they desire and stay in energetic alignment:

I call these my Shine Wellthy™ Principles, and they spell out the word WELLTHY.

W = Who are you BEING?

What energy are you in? Your state of being creates and allows you to take inspired action that propels you forward. Take 100% responsibility for your results—100% of the time—and BE the empowered six-figure coach you desire, even before you see the physical results.

E = Energy Trumps Strategy

The energy you are in will always trump the strategy you take. If you are in doubt, it will affect the actions you take. If you are feeling confident and empowered, the actions you take will work. You can't create from scarcity, no matter what strategy you use. CHOOSE what energy you want to be in—then take action.

L = Live Wealthy Now.

Choose high-vibe activities that allow you to FEEL wealthy now. How can you make an upgrade to your life that feels rich? Can you take a full hour for lunch? Nourish yourself with high-vibe foods. Get enough rest. Get a manicure or pedicure. Live wealthy NOW, and more will come to you.

L = Language of Abundance

Immerse yourself in the language of abundance. The more you practice being in abundance, the quicker it happens. What you focus on grows, so choose to focus on the abundance around you daily and OFTEN. Just like learning a foreign language—the more you speak it, the faster you learn it.

T = Track Abundance—It All Counts

Track all the ways abundance comes to you. Track all the money that comes to you—the money you find, the refunds you get. If someone takes you out for dinner or coffee, it ALL counts. Also, track the signs that show you abundance. Did someone you know have an amazing month? Track it. Acknowledge that it is possible for you, too, by saying, "I am one with that."

H = How is this working FOR me?

If something is not working out the way you think it should ask yourself this question: How is this working FOR me? List all the ways this is actually a benefit. You can also ask: How else could this go? Think of all the possible positive outcomes. Play the "what if" game from the winning side. Then, ask yourself how you can leverage this as an opportunity for something even better. Your brain loves to solve problems, so let's make sure it's focused on the right thing to solve.

Y = YES, your way to SUCCESS

EXPECT success. If you don't expect success, it can't happen. Whether you believe you can or can't, you're right. So, expect success. Look for it. Eliminate the excuses for why you can't, and take action anyway. You've got this.

You can grab your FREE Shine WELLTHY™ Cheat Sheet + Video Training inside the book portal.

I want to share how powerful this work is by sharing the story of one of my clients. I'll call her Lisa. When Lisa started working with me at Activate Abundance® Academy, she was barely paying her bills and living paycheck to paycheck from a full-time job while trying to grow her health coaching business. Her past experiences in life had handed her some pretty painful circumstances—from being addicted to drugs to being in prison to starting over in life, trying to create something she could be proud of.

But there was this voice inside that was holding her back. Who was she to think she could create fabulous success and be well-paid to help others, given her past trauma? We all have this mean girl voice inside telling us we are not good enough, smart enough, thin enough, rich enough, healed enough—the list goes on and on. And it's this voice that keeps us struggling, playing safe, and staying small.

So, she began creating a new identity—one where she saw herself as capable, powerful, and resilient and where she could use her past experiences to help others instead of letting them define her. She went through the daily alignment practice every morning and began to think and feel differently. She began to own her worthiness and value as a leader and claimed for herself being a six-figure health coach—even before the money was in the bank as "proof."

Soon, she was bringing in new clients at her highest VIP rate. She started a podcast. She created a group program in addition to her one-on-one offerings and had her first $100,000 year. She has gone on to create consistent $10,000+ months. She continues to serve women in her coaching practice and is a best-selling author, sharing her story of addiction and recovery to help more women build resilience in their lives.

All that came from the inner mindset work of aligning with the future version of herself she desired to be. She believed she could, and she did!

And if you have not yet gone through the questions above, please pause here and take time to do so. I promise you that the insights that come out of this exercise will be powerful in your future success.

In this chapter, you learned:

- The inner game of building a soulfully aligned and profitable business.

- The energy and mindset that attract abundance to you.

• The components of a daily alignment practice and belief plan that will fast-track your success because you're focused on and energetically aligning with your desires.

• The Shine Wellthy® principles of alignment that will accelerate your growth in business and life.

Next, let's dive into your Soul-Aligned STRATEGY.

Chapter 3

"The most difficult thing is the decision to act; the rest is merely tenacity." — **Amelia Earhart**

Step One ALIGN

ALIGN to your Soulmate Client and your Unique Brilliance

Inner Game *(Mindset + Energetic Alignment)* + **Outer Game** (Strategy + Inspired Action) = **ABUNDANCE**

Outer Game: Align to your Heart. Your YES Clients and YOUR unique brilliance

In the last chapter, we aligned with the INNER GAME—the mindset, energy, and feeling state that allows us to take action. Now, let's dive into the inspired actions that make up the OUTER GAME of your heart-aligned strategy. This is the YANG to the YIN—the working structure that allows you to flow in your business.

I like to use the analogy of a riverbank. Without the riverbank, the river has no direction. It just seeps into the earth, never arriving at the ocean because there is no structure to guide the flow. But with the riverbank, there is a clear direction for where the water is headed. Sure, obstacles pop up along the way, but the direction is set. The flow of the water can continue moving forward around the obstacles because it has a guiding boundary to contain it.

That's what we want our strategy to do—to guide the direction and provide specific guideposts for what to focus on every day, every week, every month, and every quarter so that you know you are headed in the right direction. Otherwise, you're just chasing bright, shiny tactics that take you nowhere. And that serves no one. You are here for a purpose, and you have it in your heart to impact others. So, let's get you there as simply and easefully as possible.

Specifically, in this chapter, we are going to identify your HEART-YES clients and uncover your unique brilliance. Everything else is created from these foundational pieces.

Inner Game (Mindset + Energetic Alignment) + **Outer Game (Strategy + Inspired Action) = ABUNDANCE**

Before we can create your six-figure plan or attract your heart-yes clients, we need to know WHO they are and what makes YOU the best person to serve them. Clarity in the outer game of uncovering your ideal client and your unique brilliance will make the rest of the strategy work quicker and easier and help establish confidence.

Your clients want to feel understood, and they want to feel important.

They seek a heartfelt connection, and YOU are the one to gift it to them.

However, you can't understand them or make them feel important until you know WHO they are, WHERE they are, WHAT they want, and HOW you can serve them in the best way possible.

When you truly understand your clients' needs, you attract them in much more emotionally compelling ways. I know from experience, and I can tell you that hearing someone speak our language is like coming home. You will feel like you belong, and in turn, you will enter your interactions with greater confidence and satisfaction.

And the cool thing is this doesn't need to be a time-heavy process. But it does require you to look at some patterns and common denominators that your heart-yes clients share.

Success leaves clues. You will hear me say this a lot. It really is true. Let's uncover the clues that will lead to your heart-yes clients.

Take a moment and work on some inspired action by following the steps below to identify your heart-yes clients.

Step 1: Make a list of your top three clients—the ones you wish you had a sold-out practice of.

These are clients you feel excited about serving. You feel joyful around them, and they show up for themselves and implement what you teach them. If you don't have any paying clients yet, imagine three people you would most LOVE to work with. You can even make them up. What would they all have in common that would make you SO excited to get out of bed in the morning to help them?

You can also interview 5–10 people who you think might be a good fit for your services. By interviewing people who might align with your offerings, you are conducting market research to uncover the specific type of person you are looking for.

Make a note of what characteristics these people share.

Are they male or female?

What is their age?

What is their occupation?

What hobbies do they take part in?

What challenges have they overcome, or are trying to overcome?

What words do they use to describe these challenges?

What words do they use to describe the solution they want to have?

Where do they go when they leave the house?

Where do they shop?

Where do they spend money?

What do they wish for?

What is important to them in the world?

Why is this important to them?

Ask quality questions that dig deep, and pay attention to the answers. Take good notes so you can refer back to them. By knowing these things, you can powerfully serve clients in the way you intend.

These questions give you insights into WHO this client is and WHERE to find them. Doing this NOW will save you many wasted hours, days, and even weeks trying to figure it out from scratch—or save you the frustration of putting together a program that does not provide the solution your clients are looking for.

When I did the exercise I'm sharing with you, so much opened up for me. I went from continuously asking myself, "Who do I serve?" to feeling certain, confident, and excited that I finally had direction in my business.

My business changed when I took a look at the top three clients I was serving in my health coaching business. All three were women. One was a health coach, one was a life coach, and one worked in the corporate world and wanted to leave it to do work that felt more fulfilling. Her goal was to help people with their health and wellness by opening up a wellness center. Prior to doing this exercise and uncovering WHO my ideal clients were, I was mostly speaking to women over forty who were struggling with burnout.

After this exercise, I realized my ideal client was a previous version of ME. She was a wellness entrepreneur—specifically, a service-based coach or holistic practitioner. It was like a light bulb went off. Once I thought of my ideal client as a previous version of me, I really understood who she was, what her desires were, what challenges she faced, and what her life and business looked like when those challenges were solved. Once I understood that, speaking to my ideal client didn't require a hot hook, an elevator pitch, or even staying within my niche.

When my client Jennifer, who is a life coach, went through this process, she was so excited to find crystal clarity that her heart-yes client wanted more than just a happy life. She wanted to thrive through grief. She was able to uncover that what her client REALLY wanted was to find serenity in the midst of the grief process. And that her story of losing a loved one—and the process she went through to come out on the other side thriving—was what made her uniquely suited to serve clients in their pain.

This clarity gave her confidence in creating her 90-day coaching program, where she guides women through the healing process. It allows her to speak to the specific problems her clients say they struggle with and self-identify with. This new level of confidence resulted in her being more visible online so potential clients could find her. This led to her connecting and collaborating with other practitioners, getting booked on summits and podcasts, and building her own Facebook community where she could share value and build and nurture relationships online.

When you go through the Soulful Abundance System®, your first month's focus is spent on the Outer Game. Everything you do moving forward will be created from the information we uncover here, so please don't skip this step.

This process is not just about picking a niche or coming up with an elevator pitch or a unique selling proposition (USP). This process is about understanding the client you are most meant to serve. Once you do, your niche becomes clear. You take all the commonalities and put them together to make ONE Heart-Yes client avatar—one that we know intimately so your energy and your message resonate with the pain and solutions your client wants help with.

This creates harmony, clarity, focus, and specificity for future programs, pricing of programs, messaging, and planning out the client pathway.

When my client Jane went through this process, she realized that her clients were all struggling with the side effects of Epstein-Barr Syndrome—a common virus that remains dormant in most people. Epstein-Barr virus causes infectious mononucleosis and has been associated with certain cancers, including Burkitt lymphoma, immunoblastic lymphoma, nasopharyngeal cancer, and stomach (gastric) cancer. Also called EBV.

When she realized this, she was able to get crystal clear on how she could help them the most. Her ideal client avatar went from a broad version of helping women get healthy to helping women who were struggling with the side effects of EBV. She talked about those side effects and became the go-to expert in helping women discover solutions tailored specifically for them.

It became easy for her to talk about her solutions because she intimately knew the problems her clients were struggling with and the missing pieces she could supply to them that would help them quickly.

Getting specific here, like my clients Jennifer and Jane, will help you ensure your messaging, programs, pricing, and offers to attract the right clients—those who are ready and willing to invest in their transformation and want you to be the one to help them. It's much easier to attract a client and serve someone powerfully than to try to convince or persuade a potential client that they need you. We don't chase down clients. We identify with them. We help them feel seen and heard. We cultivate relationships and help them self-identify that they need our support when we are clear.

Remember that this is a process. There is no need for perfection—this is just a starting place. You will uncover more and more about your soulmate clients the more you serve them, listen to them, and hear what is coming up for them. But it is important to start. So let go of the procrasti-planning and just dive in to see what you can find. Let it be a fun game. Play detective. You really can't get this wrong.

Now, onto you and your unique brilliance. This piece is super fun! When you uncover what is attractive about you and why clients are seeking you out, you can stay aligned with who you authentically are. This allows you to be a stand-out leader in your market. Later on, we will uncover what your Signature System is to support your clients in getting from Pain Island to Pleasure Island—but for this exercise, we want to focus on what makes you special.

To help you with this piece, I like to use a quiz called The Soul of Your Brand. It's a quick way to uncover your brand archetype and what's most attractive about you to your ideal clients. There are 12 brand archetypes, and your top two determine the soul of your brand. It's the inner magic that makes you, well, you—and it is incredibly attractive to the clients who want to work with you. Your brand archetype captures your spirit, personality, and passion, pulling it together into a neat, captivating, and authentic brand you can use for marketing and client attraction. From your marketing message to your website, you can leverage your unique brilliance as a powerful catalyst to grow your business.

Your ideal clients see in you what they would like more of. When you uncover your top two archetypes, you'll recognize what's been with you all along and gain a deeper understanding of how to use your unique strengths confidently and authentically to build a brand your clients trust. This also ensures that you create a brand that feels fully aligned with who you are and what you value.

Brand archetypes are based on psychology and convey deeper meaning beyond just the individual words used to describe them. They access something profound within us. Psychologist Carl Jung formalized the modern concept of archetypes in the early 1900s, though some scholars trace the roots of the concept all the way back to Plato.

There are 12 Brand Archetypes.

- The Ruler - Creates order, peace and prosperity

- The Sage - seeks to understand the world around us and share knowledge

- The Romantic- Deepens intimacy and connections

- The Nurturer- Creates meaning by caring for others

- The Innocent - Renews our faith in the simple, pure and gentle

- The Explorer- Searches for authentic meaning and leaves their unique mark in the world

- The Artist - Awakens the inner creator and imagination

- The Hero- Triumphs over adversity and takes courageous action

- The Humanitarian - Believes in the common good for all

- The Alchemist - Creates transformation and possibility

- The Maverick – is a rule breaker and challenges the world as we know it

- The Jester - Offers a different and playful perspective

These brand archetypes were created and introduced to me by one of my mentors, Kendall SummerHawk. She is the original creator of using brand archetypes to help coach other women in building and growing their businesses in a way that feels authentic, aligned for entrepreneurs, and attractive to clients.

To discover what your Signature and Influencing Archetypes [2] are, go to this link, where you can find the Branding with Archetypes® quiz: https://learn.shineabundancenow.com/branding-with-archetypes.

Let's take a closer look at each archetype.

- **The Ruler: Creates peace, order, and prosperity.**

The Ruler's mission is to create a structure so others can prosper. Though you may often be quiet, if you scored high as

---

[2] Selected portions of these materials have been legally licensed from the copyright owner, Heart of Success, Inc. Copyright 2024 Heart of Success, Inc.

The Ruler, you are often commanding, authoritative, and have little patience for ambiguity. The Ruler archetype appeals to our desire to feel important, in control, and in charge. Ruler brands help us become the King, Queen, or Goddess of our domain. While the Ruler can seem domineering or autocratic, their true gift is in empowering leadership, prosperity, and success in others.

Your Ruler brand appeals to those who want to feel secure, get organized, and believe what they need has already been thought out for them—by them. They want things to be under control and to feel a sense of mastery. The Ruler brand archetype appeals to the desire to feel significant and important, and those drawn to it want a leader they can trust, admire, and be inspired by. The branding has a feeling of grace and power. The Ruler has a natural ability to organize things into systems that make clients feel appreciated, valued, and important. Everyone wants to feel successful, and the Ruler brand is ideal for inspiring confidence and creating clients who will be loyal to you for life!

Some powerful branding words to use in your copy and messaging—and to help you choose images that resonate with clients looking for The Ruler brand—are:

Power, Decision, Strength, Ideal, Command, Confidence, Trust, Sacred, Order, Chaos, Authority, Established, Focus, Organized, Should, Super, High-powered, Privileged, Exclusive, Elite, Harmony, Important, Limit, Security, Priority, Prestige, First-class, Control, Impressive, Mastery, Influence, Wealth,

Dominate, Lead, Image, Success, Safety, Flawless, Law, Rule/Rules, Prosperity, Build, Timeless, Status, Protect, Benevolence, All, Empire, Money.

- **The Romantic: Creates deeper connections.**

If you scored high as The Romantic archetype, your primary drive is finding and giving love. The Romantic archetype's deep desire is for intimacy, connection, and feeling singled out as special. The Romantic covers the spectrum from pure sexuality to enduring love to deep friendship. The Romantic is attentive, often elegant, and promises a feeling of being loved, desired, indulged, or decadent. The Romantic archetype appeals to one's core need to be loved and appreciated. The enduring quality of the Romantic appeals to a deep longing for the ideal relationship.

The Romantic brand appeals to those who crave a deeper sensory experience and heartfelt connection. They desire to feel loved and special, and they want to be romanced. They love secrets, flirting, and attention. They crave feeling like they are the center of your world and are often willing to pay a premium for this type of specialness. Give your branding a high-touch feel, and be sure to include surprises that will delight their senses. Everyone wants to feel loved, and if your Romantic brand treats your clients as a cherished friend or lovers, they will appreciate your care with loyalty and commitment!

Some powerful branding words to use in your copy and messaging—and images that resonate with clients looking for The Romantic brand—are:

Romance, Heart, Sex, Desire, Friendship, Beauty, Connection, Adored, Magnetism, Resist, Attract, Seduction, Deep, Elegant, Tantalize, Envy, Tempting, Power, Allure, Appeal, Guilty, Emotion, Erotic, Pleasures, Animal, Love, Moonlight, Relationship, Intimacy, Luscious, Indulge, Caring, Passion, Quality, Secrets, Forever, Appreciated, Commitment, Attention, Special, Thoughtful.

• **The Nurturer: Offers generosity, caring, and compassion that help clients feel at home**.

If you scored high as The Nurturer archetype, you care for others' health, happiness, and well-being by soothing hurts and comforting hearts. The Nurturer's deep desire is to take care of the people and things in their world, keeping them safe and protected. While often associated with women ("Mother Earth"), men, too, can claim this role. Although they are not typically the center of attention, the Nurturer's influence can be felt throughout our society and its social programs. The Nurturer appeals to our need for comfort and acceptance, no matter what.

The Nurturer brand appeals to those who desire to feel cared for, protected, or comforted. Those drawn to The Nurturer brand crave safety, both physical and emotional. They want to feel valued, appreciated and accepted as they are. Establish in your branding that you are a safe haven, making sure your clients feel your caring, compassion, and generosity in every aspect of your business. Everyone wants to feel secure and loved, and your Nurturer brand can easily create an environment

Christine Williams appears top.

where clients feel their needs and feelings are important. When you make them the center of your world, they will love you for life!

Some powerful branding words to use in your copy and messaging, as well as images that resonate with clients looking for The Nurturer, are:

Care, Others, Protect, Stewardship, Soothe, Cherish, Benefit, Compassion, Support, Attentive, Sacrifice, Mother Nature, Connecting, Touch, Compelled, Dependable, Empathy, Safety, Health, Happiness, Devoted, Giving, Generous, Helpful, Intuitive, Kind, Good, Worry, Constancy, Love, Trust, Provide, Listening, Positive, Sensitive, Nourish, Comfort, Reliable, Hope, Satisfy, Unconditional, Understanding, Grow, Thoughtful, Family.

• The Innocent: Renews our faith in the simple, innocent, and gentle.

The promise of The Innocent is that we can be happy. If you score high as The Innocent archetype, your childlike appeal touches the heart and holds out hope that somehow, we can escape the hectic life around us and instead find ourselves in our own version of Utopia. The Innocent's unwavering faith and optimism speak to a need for simpler times, wholesomeness, and honest values. Innocent brands create long-lasting loyalty because there is always some part of us that wants to either be a kid again or feel taken care of in at least one corner of our lives. No matter how practical the product is, when it is created by

The Innocent archetype, it becomes something that makes us smile, feel good, and be hopeful about the world again.

The Innocent brand appeals to those who desire an escape to something simpler, better, or gentler. They love feeling a childlike wonder. They love feeling sentimental or even wistful for days gone by. They desire to relinquish all responsibility for at least a brief period. They crave feeling fresh, renewed, and made new again. Create in your branding a feeling of escape, simplicity, and ease. Include a sense of happiness, dreaminess, or childlike optimism. Everyone wants to feel rejuvenated, and The Innocent brand can easily be positioned as a sanctuary where peace and simplicity are abundant!

Some powerful branding words to use in your copy and messaging, as well as images that resonate with clients looking for you, are:

Wonder, Child, Pure, Dreamy, White, New, Fresh, Clear, Faith, Simple, Uncomplicated, Good, Organic, Nature, Happiness, Eden, Tender, Clean, Wholesome, Real, Harmony, Heaven-sent, Renew, Safe, Ideal, Honesty, Authenticity, Upbeat, Optimistic, Perfect, Supported, Promise, Protected, Paradise, Idyllic, Cute, Playful.

- **The Explorer: Searches for authentic meaning.**

If you score high as The Explorer archetype, your drive is to seek new experiences. You have a foot in both the physical and spiritual world, as you see both as landscapes of possibilities and self-expression. Restless and often ambitious, the Explorer's quest is for individuality and uniqueness. You often feel alone (since you are usually out in front, blazing a trail) and shy away from depending on others. Your intense need for wide-open vistas and what is new or different keeps you on the move. For this reason, Explorers comfortably embrace different cultures and ideas. Your deeply rooted need for self-expression and individuality gives us a positive role model for discovering our own unique brilliance and originality.

The Explorer brand appeals to those who want to feel free and true to themselves. They crave creating their unique mark on the world and look to you for tools and solutions to help them reach this highly personal goal. They want to feel unique and special. The Explorer brand appealed to a time in their life when they desired to express their authentic individuality. Give your branding a positive, ambitious, goal-achieving orientation, and let it reflect that the journey is just as important as the destination. Everyone has a desire to discover new insights about themselves and live by their values, making your Explorer brand the perfect catalyst for creating freedom, self-expression, and independence!

Some powerful branding words to use in your copy, messaging, and images that resonate with clients looking for The Explorer are:

Unique, Individual, Signature, Travel, Genuine, Inspire, Spirit, Explore, Quest, Seek, Find, Innovate, Create, Meet, Independent, Freedom, Authentic, Identity, Non-conforming, Personal, New, Beauty, Pioneer, Soul, Journey, Destination,

Lead, Express, Fantasy, Bold, Original, Restless, Custom, Expression, Different, Depth, Discovery, Choice, Your Way, Unusual.

 • **The Artist: Turns the ordinary into the extraordinary.**

If you scored high as The Artist archetype, you are fueled by a deep desire to make things different than they are. Your imagination and unwillingness to conform are the catalysts for innovation and a never-ending stream of possibilities. What we see as simply lumps of clay, bits of paint and canvas, bricks and mortar, or untapped potential, the Artist sees as unlimited potential to transform the human experience. Your love of beauty, design, and creativity can be expressed in any form, from great art to redesigning everyday tasks and objects and even recreating our lives. You lift us up and give us permission to create not only how we see our world but also who we are in it.

The Artist brand appeals to those who are looking for their inner Creator to be awakened. They desire reinvention and want to feel the thrill of putting their unique stamp on something. They desire to feel self-expressed and valued as individuals. Your clients may not have your inventive skills or abilities, but they want to be involved in the process of creating or customizing something just for them. Give your branding a self-expressive design feel with lots of emotionally evocative imagery and encouraging, imaginative language. Everyone has an inner artist in them, and the Artist brand is the perfect catalyst for helping clients express something personal and meaningful!

Some powerful branding words to use in your copy, messaging, and images that resonate with clients looking for The Artist are:

Beauty, Art, Spirit, Portrait, Design, Craft, Elegant, Taste, Inspire, Timeless, Creativity, Imaginative, Different, Quality, Talent, Inspiration, Expression, Valued, Priceless, Treasured, Express, Unusual, Innovate, Authentic, Curiosity, Transformative, Fantasy, Vision, Do-it-yourself, Personal, Fine, Unique, Custom, Option, Daydream, Different.

- **The Hero: Triumphs over adversity and takes courageous action.**

If you score high for the Hero Archetype, your bravery and courage can take many forms, from toughness, conquest, and the drive to battle to championing those who cannot stand up for themselves. You find strength in adversity and value resilience, honor, and ambition. Your journey may be a physical one or an interior quest to prove worth, face fear, and overcome great obstacles. While your power and strength are often channeled into extreme competitiveness when directed toward a higher good, your perseverance, grit, and determination inspire us with the courage to achieve more than we thought possible. No matter what, you help us tap into our own sense of honor, values, and conviction.

The Hero brand appeals to those who want to be championed to better their best. They want to be saved from struggle or difficulties and will often seek you out when they feel most vulnerable. They crave feeling protected by strength and toughness. They want to feel the thrill of victory and achievement. Give your branding a feeling of durability, power, and winning, and include a dose of humility and vulnerability. Everyone wants to feel like a winner, and the Hero brand is ideal for helping your clients break through limits and achieve more than they previously thought possible!

Some powerful branding words to use in your copy, messaging, and images that resonate with clients looking for The Hero are:

Heroic, Destiny, Ambitious, Conquer, Courage, Victim, Skill, Purpose, Challenge, Struggle, Overcome, Triumph, Decisive, Mission, Champion, Winner, Obstacle, Victory, Loyal, Fortitude, Ambition, Tough, Strength, Discipline, Focus, Determination, Respect, Rescue, Honor, Humility, Powerful, Spirit, Resilience, Sacrifice, Conviction, Brave, Sustain, Energy, Mastery, Value, Journey, Surrender, Achieve.

• **The Humanitarian: Stands up for the common good.**

The Humanitarian archetype is the unsung hero. If you scored high as The Humanitarian, your preference is to work behind the scenes for what you believe is fair and just, though you are willing to take center stage for a cause that is important enough to you. You want to ensure the common person feels heard, recognized, and valued. In your "I'm just like you" style, you are often the driving force behind great social change. You lead from the trenches, often inspiring others with your simple, forthright character. The Humanitarian archetype taps into the desire to know that we all count and that we each have a voice, no matter our status in life.

The Humanitarian brand appeals to those who desire a sense of belonging, just as they are. They crave friendship and connection and value everyday honest qualities over elite status. They want to feel allegiance and love, showing their affiliation by wearing clothes or symbols that represent their association with a brand or team. Establish in your branding that you are a friend, sharing common, down-to-earth values of goodness, friendliness, and neighborly caring, ensuring you never put on airs. Give them something they can wear to show their connection with you. Everyone wants to feel they belong, and your Humanitarian brand can easily create a long-lasting bond of loyalty and friendship with your clients!

Some powerful branding words to use in your copy, messaging, and images that resonate with clients looking for you are:

Fairness, Equal, Old-fashioned, Fit in, Diversity, Common, Acceptance, Ordinary, Reliable, Crowd, Everyday, Friendly, Inclusive, Connection, Folk, Genuine, Community, Alliance, Utilitarian, Honest, No-nonsense, Real, Unassuming, Integrity, Character, Simple, Regular, Same, Earthy, Good, Neighbor, Underdog, Group, Belong, Support, Union, Average, Frugal, Everybody Likes.

• The Alchemist: Makes dreams come true through transformations and inspires possibility.

If you score high as The Alchemist archetype, you are the visionary, catalyst, innovator, charismatic leader, mediator, shaman, healer, or medicine man or woman. You inspire people to commit to a higher vision of what they can be or do. Your services promise transformation and often have the allure of instant change. Although Alchemist brands like Weight Watchers produce slower transformations, there is still a marked contrast between where a person starts and where they end up. You love synchronicity, are unconventional and hopeful, and value the link between magic and practical outcomes. The Alchemist appeals to our desire to snap our fingers and experience a sense of magic, transforming ourselves or our situation into what we dream it can be.

Your Alchemist brand appeals to those who desire something in their lives to be magically transformed. They crave change in areas important to them and want you to make it easy for them to reach their goal. This is the essence of making change feel magical. They love anything that feels new or amazing and are attracted to things mystical or ancient in origin. They will look to you to help them realize their dream, give them a clear vision, or help them see a new possibility. Make sure your branding takes a specific desire and presents it in a way that feels transformational. Everyone wants to feel wowed by something magical, and the Alchemist brand is ideal for helping people feel that what they want is possible!

Some powerful branding words to use in your copy, messaging, and images that resonate with clients looking for you are:

Magic, Transformation, Visionary, Mystery, Fascinating, Dream, Ritual, Mind/Body, Change, Essence, Manifestation, Power, Catalyst, Enlightening, Hunch, Disguise, Miracle, Manifest, Intuition, Universe, Instant, Chemistry, Synchronicity, Flow, Influence, Charisma, Before/After, Spirit, Breakthrough, Change, Appear, Energy, Simple/Complex, Wisdom, Fantasy, Transform, Play, Escape, Potential.

- **The Maverick: Challenges the world as we know it and is the rule breaker.**

The Maverick is driven to shake things up. If you scored high as The Maverick archetype, you are likely the rebel, outlaw, daredevil, or revolutionary. You may feel like an alienated outsider, yet you often possess a romantic "bad boy" identity that is highly charismatic. Your power to transform is through disruption, breaking the rules, and challenging authority. Your need to revolt is a powerful force behind important social change, yet it can also swing to lawlessness and even the victimization of others. Mavericks such as the mythic Bonnie and Clyde or Butch Cassidy and the Sundance Kid give the rest of us permission to express our dark side—that part that yearns to break loose, challenge limits, or participate in forbidden behavior.

The Maverick brand appeals to those who want to feel free, rebellious, or bad—even if just temporarily. They desire to stand out from the crowd or to be part of a cause in a revolutionary way. They want to leave responsibility behind (even if just for the weekend). You appeal to their desire to stop conforming. They want to feel different from others or from what is traditionally done in their life. Give your branding edgy images and copywriting that describe feeling liberated, rebellious, or fighting for a cause. Everyone has a wild side, and the Maverick brand is the catalyst to bring out their inner rebel!

Some powerful branding words to use in your copy, messaging, and images that resonate with clients looking for The Maverick are:

Break, Rebel, Adolescent, Danger, Attention, Revolutionary, Shock, Struggle, Silver-Tongued Devil, Authority, Edgy, Contrary, Wild, Defiance, Vicarious, Misfit, Sexuality, Bold, Freedom, Thrill, Challenge, Counter, Daring, Fight, Outlaw, Forbidden, Rights, Outrageous, Defy, Different, Injustice, Attitude, Disregard, Extreme, Against.

• The Jester: Offers a different perspective and inspires imagination.

If you score high as the Jester archetype, you are never satisfied with the status quo. You use your cleverness to help those around you see the world from a new perspective. Your love of the unexpected jars us out of complacency and reminds us not to take life too seriously. You may sometimes have a disrespect for what is proper, which often puts you at odds with the "powers that be." Yet, by doing so, you create the possibility for a variety of new ideas and innovations to be expressed.

The Jester gives us permission to, at times, be a little naughty, have fun, and escape from our daily cares and responsibilities. By making fun of anything and everything, you help us relax and add fun, spontaneity, and enjoyment into the predictability of our lives.

The Jester brand appeals to those who desire to have fun and escape everyday issues. They love to laugh, desire variety and are always looking for novelty. They want to be surprised and love seeing how silly others can be. They want you to help them tap into their youthful, playful side and love to feel a little naughty. Make sure your branding is fresh, colorful, and takes a playful approach. Everyone wants to have more fun, and the Jester brand is ideal for helping people lighten up and laugh, no matter how difficult their challenges may be!

- **The Sage: Discovers the truth and shares wisdom.**

The Sage archetype is driven to search for information, wisdom, and insight and to share these with the rest of the world. If you scored high as The Sage archetype, you are a natural skeptic and seek to find proof or evidence to validate your discoveries, insights, or hypotheses. At your best, you integrate information and insight to uplift our spirit and advance our lives. When expressing your gifts, you are able to uncover true wisdom from the merely factual. You value experience, advice, and legacy.

The Sage appeals to our desire for rationale, logic, and explanations to support insights. The Sage brand appeals to those who desire information they can trust and believe. They crave receiving information and then making up their own minds. They want to feel validated and that their opinions are respected. They value empathy and want to know you've been in their shoes so they can learn the steps you took to go from struggle to success.

Establish in your branding that you are an expert, giving plenty of proof that your information can be trusted, and always show the pros and cons of working with you. Use knowledge-based tools, such as writing a book or creating a course, to show your expertise. Everyone is hungry to increase their knowledge and abilities, and your Sage brand can easily be positioned as a trusted source that your ideal clients respect and admire!

Some powerful branding words to use in your copy, messaging, and images that resonate with clients looking for The Sage are:

Establish, Mastery, Wisdom, Knowledge, Study, Learn, Academic, Proof, Lesson, Expert, Data, Contemplate, Elite, Information, Objectivity, Analyze, Intelligence, Plan, Reliable, Investigate, Research, Believe, Independence, Think, Respect, Experience, Mentor, Harmony, Tutorial, Understanding, Advice, Trust, Honor, Curiosity.

When we dive into brand archetypes, we look at not just one but two of your top archetypes. This creates a beautiful depth of what you are uniquely bringing to the world. We call these your Signature Archetype and your Influencing Archetype. Together, they will help you create the SOUL of your brand. This information will help you answer the questions: Who am I?

What do I stand for? What am I an expert in or at? And what feelings do your heart-yes clients want to have by being in your world? These answers, along with the archetype descriptions, will help you create the feeling and tone of all your marketing materials, big and small—from website design to messaging, to the images you share on social media, and the copy you develop. They all work together to create a congruent brand.

For example, you can create copy to use on social media, in blog posts, or in your emails that incorporate the branding words of your Signature and Influencing Archetypes. Doing this will convey the feeling and message that are most attractive to your clients. Adding a photo that aligns with your branding words will evoke the feelings you want your potential clients to have. Doing so will put you "ON BRAND" with the soul of your message.

If you are an Alchemist archetype, you would want to talk about transformation and helping others see the possibilities of their dreams. Then, you would want to share an image or photo that represents that dream, result, or outcome of the transformation they desire. When you create a webpage or website, you will do the same thing. Using the branding words of your top two archetypes, you can speak to the challenges your client might be facing and then paint a picture—with both words and images—of the results that are possible when working with you. You can see an example of this on my homepage, ShineAbundanceNow.com. Notice how the photos and words are congruent with each other and create a meaningful picture of what's possible when you work with me. By the way, I am a Ruler archetype with an Influencing Alchemist.

Another example is when you decide on the fonts to use with your brand. If you are a Jester archetype, you would want your font to be playful. If you are an Innocent archetype, you would want the font to be simple and clear—easy to read. If you are a Romantic, your font might be cursive, flowing, and more luxurious.

Brand archetypes are especially powerful for attracting heart-yes clients because they connect deeply with fundamental aspects of human psychology. When we align with our own unique combination, we can show up more authentically, attract more paying clients, and effectively communicate how we can serve the clients we are here to impact. This intuitive understanding is exactly the power we're looking to tap into.

Just like our fingerprints, we each have a unique code—a combination of our top two brand archetypes. Together, they define your unique brilliance and what naturally attracts people to you. When my client Anna went through this process at a "Soul of Your Brand" workshop I offered, she was blown away by the clarity she walked away with.

Anna was feeling confused and discouraged about how she could stand out in her niche as a mindfulness and transformation coach. She knew it was important to be clear in her messaging so she could attract the right clients into her ecosystem, but she felt stuck.

After going through my "Soul of Your Brand" workshop, she uncovered that her Signature Archetype was The Alchemist, and her Influencing Archetype was The Romantic. As The Alchemist, she was a charismatic visionary and innovator. As The Romantic, she created deep connections with people. When she uncovered this, she finally felt like she had come home to herself. She proudly and confidently stood up, knowing exactly what to say and what made her process unique and valuable to her potential clients.

She realized that she could naturally take complex and mystical ideas, such as mindfulness and meditation, and make them easy and practical for her clients to understand. She had been doing this all along but hadn't realized it was special to her until she discovered her Alchemist Brand Archetype. In fact, when we talked about some of her past experiences, she shared that she had spent about four years at an ashram studying mindfulness and meditation.

Using this information, I helped Anna design her signature framework so she could easily communicate how her clients could transform their stressful lives into the fulfilling and peaceful lives they craved by working with her. She walked out of the workshop with a clear, on-brand marketing plan that felt authentic to her and attractive to her ideal clients. Now, when she talks about what she does, she speaks with purpose and confidence. She's clear on what words attract her soulmate clients, how to communicate her message effectively to convey the feelings she wants, and what is so special about her that her "right" client would be asking for more.

Christine Williams

Every client in the workshop shared their excitement about the insights they gained while they were there. They felt empowered, clear, and confident about what made them unique and empowered in how to communicate their uniqueness in a way that was on-brand for each of them. This gave them such a sense of relief that they didn't have to try to be anybody other than who they are. That is priceless.

By learning about brand archetypes, you have some foundational pieces of the Outer Game to design your six-figure business:

- Who your soulmate client is?

- What your soulmate client is looking for?

- What makes YOU the one to meet their needs in a way that is authentically and brilliantly YOU?

Hold onto this information for later. We will be using it to help you build an audience and community who want what you have to share and are looking for your support.

In this chapter, you learned:

- The outer strategy of aligning with your ideal client and WHO they are.

- What your ideal client is looking for.

• How uncovering your brand archetypes helps you build a strong SOUL of your brand, allowing you to be authentically you and attract heart-yes clients who are looking for you, resonate with you, and are the ones you want to work with.

• Words to use in your messaging and copy, along with photos that work well to bring clients into your ecosystem.

In the next chapter, we'll design the remaining foundational pieces of your six-figure business.

Your next steps:

1. Take some time to explore who your heart-YES client is—not just their age and demographic, but what they really want. What are their fears and struggles? What wakes them up at night? What problem feels so big and important that they are ready to solve it now? And once they have solved it, what is the outcome and result they want? How does it impact their lives, relationships, quality of life, work, spirituality, and health?

2. Take the Soul of Your Brand quiz in the book portal and find out what is unique about you that draws your clients into your world.

3. Make a list of all the things you have done, achieved, and moved through that give you credibility and authority to serve clients in your chosen field. And yes, your personal process through it all counts.

Chapter 4
Step 2 Design

"One of the most courageous things you can do is identify yourself, know who you are, what you believe in, and where you want to go." — **Sheila Murray Bethel.**

Now, we get to the actual creation of what you want your business to look and function like. In this step, we will first create clarity around your VISION for your business and lifestyle. Then, we can create the practical systems to accomplish your goals.

Remember our formula:

Inner Game (mindset + energetic alignment) + Outer Game (strategy + implementation) = Abundance.

Let's dive into the Inner Game (mindset + energetic alignment) of the Design Step:

For transformation to occur, we need to know, see, and feel what it is we want to be experiencing. Many times, we know what we don't want but are not sure what we do want. Vision Casting is a combination of what we want to experience and the measure to know when we have it. It's not just something to work toward; it's the mindset we come from to create what we want.

When both are aligned with each other, we stay inspired and in action. Traditional goal-setting methods typically lack one or both of these components.

Think about your life, personally and professionally, as of late. Have you set some recent goals?

- Did you create the results that you wanted?

- If not, what got in the way?

- If you did create results, what worked?

Find a quiet space. Start with a few moments of deep breathing or meditation to quiet your mind and allow your inner wisdom to guide you in answering these questions.

The first step in Vision Casting is to connect with the experience you desire to have. If you could wave a magic wand and really get what you want, what would that look like?

- Who are you a year from now?

- What does your life look like one year from now?

- How about three years from now?

See yourself having and living the experience that you desire. Step into this future that has already had the outcome and results you want. Be mindful of what is reasonable—statistics show that we overestimate what we can accomplish in a year and underestimate what we can accomplish in three years.

When you are imagining this, ask yourself these questions:

- Where are you?

- Who is with you?

- What are you doing?

- What thoughts are you thinking?

- How are you feeling in your body?

- What does your day look like?

- What does your week look like?

- How many clients are you working with?

- What is it like to be you?

Use all of your senses: What do you see, smell, hear, taste, feel, and know to be true?

Close your eyes and sink into this. Allow yourself to imagine living this experience, even if you don't know how it will happen. It is okay if you do not know. The goal is to take the first step and emotionally connect to what you desire.

Take some time to journal it out. What does it feel like to live this experience? Use descriptive words to bring it to life.

Create your "I AM" statement.

Your **I AM** statement is your belief. It's what you are stepping into as you bring your future self into **NOW**.
It answers the question: Who will I get to **BE** in order to have this experience of life?

An example of this is **"I AM self-assured"** or **"I AM worthy."** You can add any adjective or adjective phrase here (wise, joyful, willing to speak my truth, etc.).

I am _____.

The BIG 5

Having a profitable and sustainable business does not happen in a vacuum. The way we do one thing is the way we do everything. So, the next place we want to look at is the five big areas of life. I call these the **BIG 5**. And when we are clear on what we desire here, our business plan flows more smoothly and effortlessly.

The **BIG 5** areas of life are:

• Business/Money

• Personal Growth

• Health

- Relationships

- Spirituality

To get clear on what your **BIG 5** areas of life are, you need to ask yourself: **What is the EXPERIENCE you want to create in the BIG 5 areas of your life?**

To do this, brainstorm and identify one to three outcomes that are important to living your most successful and empowering year. Make sure that your outcomes are specific and measurable.

For example, if one of your health goals is to get more movement in, the measure of that might be to walk a certain number of days per week. If your goal is to make more money, be clear in your thoughts—how much money do you want to make by the end of the year?

Use the worksheet below to record your answers. Once you complete the worksheet, highlight the top **needle mover** in each area. In other words, what is the **ONE** thing that, when achieved, will create an empowering experience of life for each area?

BUSINESS/ MONEY: Think about your marketing, sales, and YOU. What are the areas that stand out as clearly needing to be elevated in the next year? What specifically needs attention?

Christine Williams

1.

2.

3.

PERSONAL GROWTH: Think about your mindset, beliefs, the way you see business, the way you react to things, and the way you show up in the world (who you are being). What are the areas that stand out as clearly needing to be elevated in the next year? What specifically needs attention?

1.

2.

3.

HEALTH: Think about your sleep, nutrition, water intake, exercise, energy, etc. What are the areas that stand out as clearly needing to be elevated in the next year? What specifically needs attention?

1.

2.

RELATIONSHIPS: Think about your love partnership, how you communicate, friends, relationships with family, with people in general, community. What are the areas that stand out as clearly needing to be elevated in the next year? What specifically needs attention?

1.

2.

SPIRITUALITY: Think about your connection with the Source. (Use the words that you feel most drawn to as your source. For me, it's God.) What are the areas that stand out as clearly needing to be elevated in the next year? What specifically needs attention.

1.

2.

Next, tap into your BIG WHY.

- Why is it that you want to do what you do?

- What will this allow you to do more of in your life?

- How will it affect the others around you?

Christine Williams

● What ripples do you create in this world when you are successful and serving others with your work?

I want you to see just how powerful you are and how important your work is to share with the world.

Now it's time to dive into the Outer Game (strategy + implementation) of the Design Step. This step covers the practical FOUNDATIONS of your six-figure business.

In this step, we want to uncover the systems you want to have in place and the specific ways your clients can work with you.

When you have these dialed in, you can confidently begin to attract your soulmate clients.

When I was first growing my business, I was missing the "system or process" component of the way I helped clients move from Pain Island to Pleasure Island. I knew I could help them, but I was all over the place trying to communicate what I did and why they would want to work with me over someone else.

Then I learned about creating my personal Signature System and BINGO—everything came together.

Instead of trying to sell myself, I now had a process—a series of steps that people could connect with and see that there was an actual pathway to their transformation. And the cool thing is that people WANT this structure. They want to know the steps. They desire a clear pathway, and when you have a personal process to take them through, you stand out as a leader and an in-demand coach or practitioner.

Design Your Six-Figure Signature System

Having a signature system or proprietary process is your moneymaker. It will be the game changer for creating a six- or even seven-figure business. Without this, you will just be trying to SELL yourself. The truth is that people invest in processes. They want to know you have a pathway, framework, or method to take them through so they will achieve their transformation.

Think of your Six-Figure Signature System as organizing your unique process step by step. Each step has clearly defined outcomes—or results—along the way. Your signature framework illustrates how you get your clients from where they are now (Point A) to where they want to go (Point B).

When prospective clients see the solution to their problem laid out like this, they feel understood, excited, and confident that you can help them.
You aren't just 'a coach' or 'a healer'—you have a process. This increases perceived value from the perspective of a potential client. It sets you up as the leader and expert to help them get what they desire.

The Importance of Your Six-Figure Signature System:

• Makes your expertise highly marketable

- Establishes you as a leader in your market

- Makes your expertise easy for your ideal clients to understand and want to hire you for

- Differentiates you from other coaches and practitioners

- Allows you to take the beautiful work you do with clients and put it into a sequence

- Shows the value of your offer—people invest in a PROCESS before they buy into YOU

- Makes it easy to talk about what you do

- Helps your ideal clients get excited about how you can help them

- Is a dynamic, essential element of building your business

- Is easy to create

- Is duplicable, repeatable, and scalable

- Has the potential to radically transform your business

Six-Figure Signature System Opportunities

Here are some ways that your signature system can 10X your impact, income, and visibility in your business.

1. Creating Confidence

• With your Six-Figure Signature System, you will feel calm and organized about what you do, and you will be able to talk about your services with clarity and confidence.

2. Standing Out from **the** Crowded Market

• Specializing is the key to attracting new clients. People want specialists, not generalists.

3. **Springboarding** One Idea into Multiple New Offers

• You can offer your Six-Figure Signature System in a variety of ways, giving you freedom because you're leveraging your time and your opportunities—VIP days, retreats, bite-sized offers, books, programs, and more.

4. Speaking **and** Joint Venture Opportunities

• Your Six-Figure Signature System positions you as an expert on your topic for speaking on stages, summits, podcasts, etc.

5. Easy Marketing

• Your Six-Figure Signature System inspires and organizes your copywriting, blog posts, article content, and Facebook group live.

6. Avoiding Bright Shiny Object Syndrome

• With your Six-Figure Signature System, you'll be able to stay focused on what you're offering.

7. Attracting Clients That Will Love Your Signature System

• Transforming what you do into something that looks, feels, and seems tangible is crucial. People need to see a pathway from where they are struggling to the solution.

• Your Six-Figure Signature System shows that you have figured everything out for your client. This establishes trust and confidence.

• Clients love hearing that you have a step-by-step process because it's focused on achieving a particular result. It's specific and helps them envision the transformation they desire. The enrollment process becomes about the transformation instead of just making a sale to work with you. It takes the pressure off you to **sell** yourself. Instead, you get to teach your process or method and then naturally invite someone to work with you.

Uncovering Your Six-Figure Signature System

Let's dive into how you can do this for yourself.

• Start by writing down each step or stage your client will go through when working with you and how they will know when each stage is complete. What needs to be accomplished before they go on to the next step?

• Simplify as much as possible.

• Give each step a name that is one word (a verb) that describes the action or result of the step.

• Identify three to six steps needed to get your client from pain island (the problem they are struggling with) to pleasure island (the transformation or result they desire) by using YOUR PROCESS. Your system is your process. Some other terms you may have heard this called are:

• **Unique Solution**

• **Signature System**

• **Unique Branded System**

• **Proprietary Process**

• **Method**

• **Pathway**

• **Blueprint**

• **Formula**

• **Code**

They are all basically the same thing.

Yours will typically be based on a **series of steps, a series of pillars, or a series of stages.**

Mapping out your method/system/framework:

- Stage/Step/Pillar #1: _____

Description: Example: Step one in the Soulful Abundance System is ALIGN. We energetically align with our value and worthiness as the six-figure business owner we desire to be and claim it NOW. Then, we uncover and align with our unique brilliance and the ideal client we want to work with.

What does this stage involve? What things will you be helping them with?

How do you know when it's done? What does it look like for the client when this step is complete?

Repeat this process for EACH step/stage/pillar and keep it to just 3-6 steps.

Give each step a name using an ACTION word.

For example, the Soulful Abundance System® steps are:

- ALIGN

- DESIGN

- ATTRACT

- NURTURE

- INVITE

- EMPOWER

PICK A TITLE for Your System

Spend some time coming up with a name and a description for your signature framework that is results-oriented.

Mine is **Soulful Abundance System®**. It's a six-step, simple, relational-based method to help coaches and holistic practitioners build six-figure and beyond businesses based on heart-centered values—without trading their integrity or well-being for success.

Other names that some of my clients use are:

- The Divine Profit Method

- The Launching Made Easy Framework

- The Momentum Method

- The Conviction Marketing Method

- The Posting for Profit Method, etc.

Every successful coach and entrepreneur has a **PROCESS** that they take clients through, and your framework will be **YOUR UNIQUE** process.

Once you name your system, add one of the words from the list below to the end of the title. This allows you to differentiate it as your system:

- **Method**

- **System**

- **Framework**

- **Blueprint**

- **Pathway**

- **Code**

- **Process**

- **Plan**

Next, we want to **NAME** your Six-Figure Signature System based on **RESULTS**. _____

People are looking for "what's in it for them," so the name of our system needs to resonate with the result they desire. For example, my system, the **Soulful Abundance System®**, gives the result of helping women create abundance in their business in a way that is in alignment with their soul.

Now, let's put it all together.

Create Your Six-Figure Signature System Template

Overall Title of Your Six-Figure Signature System:

_____

- **STEP 1 of Your Six-Figure Signature System**

- **STEP 2 of Your Six-Figure Signature System**

- **STEP 3 of Your Six-Figure Signature System**

- **STEP 4 of Your Six-Figure Signature System**

- **STEP 5 of Your Six-Figure Signature System**

- **STEP 6 of Your Six-Figure Signature System**

Great job! You've just created your own **proprietary** method.

Now, What to Do with Your Signature System—and How It Will 10x Your Opportunities

Get your new **Signature System** out in front of potential clients as quickly as possible. That way, you can see how people will move through it and get feedback on what may need to be adjusted.

Ideas for this include:

- Walking people through it 1:1

- Allow yourself to evolve and tweak as you go

- Make your signature system the HERO. This takes the pressure off of you needing to SELL yourself. It's the process people will want to learn.

- Adding your signature system into your marketing content and posts so people see it as much as they see you. Communicate about your framework OFTEN. Remember>> Repetition creates belief.

- Do a nurture event or training around it! (We will dive into the how-to's of a nurture event in the NURTURE chapter.)

- Write a blog post about it

- Structure your Facebook lives around it

- Talk about it on a podcast

- Share it on a virtual summit

- Create a Lead magnet around it

- Do an in-person event or talk about it

- Structure a signature and talk around it

- Share pieces of it and create a bite-size offer from it.

- Write a book about it.

The beauty of your Signature System is that it's YOURS. No one else has it. You can even trademark it like I did. Now, you have a simple process that people can understand and that YOU can use as the basis of your marketing and sales process. That's pressing the easy button!

By now, you can see why this is a game-changer for creating confidence, opportunities, and new clients. It takes the complexity of what you have in your mind for the way you help people and organizes the information so you can communicate it clearly and attract the RIGHT people into your ecosystem.

When my client Helen came up with her Signature System, she became the standout leader in her market for helping people ditch the diet and learn her "Energetic Eating Method." Now, instead of trying to "sell" people on working with her because she is an amazing coach (which she is), she has a system and a process that people can see for themselves. Her system walks them through each step to get the results they want. She is a standout leader in her field because she has a process that no one else has. It's uniquely hers. It has allowed her to sell out retreats, book more calls, be featured on podcasts, serve more clients, change lives, and have so much more FUN in her business. Just this past January, we celebrated her first $40,000 month.

Helen's simple, focused message and repeatable marketing method keep things streamlined and top of mind for her current and potential clients. And she makes six figures year after year in a much easier, more authentic, aligned, and natural way than just trying to convince strangers to become buyers.

We will dive in more on how to use this to exponentially grow your business in the future chapters.

Design your Business Model, Programs, and Pricing with a Six-Figure Playbook.

There are so many ways you can create six figures. In this section, we will focus on how YOU want your business to actually get you six figures.

Business Model

Your business model is how you want to deliver your services. We want to keep it simple and focused on the services and how you deliver them in a way that LIGHTS you up.

How do you like to conduct your business?

- Do you like running groups?

- Do you like working 1:1 with clients?

- Do you like online events or in-person events?

Once you know how you best enjoy delivering services, you can design VIP days, weekend retreats, virtual events, collaborations, and so many other products to bring income into your business.

Since my focus is on service-based wellness coaches or holistic practitioners, I'll share with you the common models they choose.

The top TWO ways my clients like to serve are either in a 1:1 format or in small groups. And some, like me, offer a hybrid model of the two.

I Like BOTH groups and 1:1 containers. I like BOTH virtual experiences and in-person ones. So, I created my model to focus on the ways I most LOVE to serve and the experience I get to give and have with my people.

When you are on your way to six figures, it is best to focus on TWO core offers for your business and a mini bite-size offer to help people get to know you.

Here are three examples of core offers that have been the most effective for my clients.

- **Model 1:**

- *High Tier offer:* 90-day 1:1 Coaching program

- *Middle Tier offer:* Group Program (six weeks- 12 weeks)

- *Bite Size offer:* One-Hour blueprint session

- **Model 2:**

- *High Tier offer:* High-End Group Coaching Program with some 1:1 access. (12 weeks- One year)

- *Middle Tier offer:* Intro Group Program (four to six weeks)

- *Bite Size offer:* One-hour blueprint session or assessment

- **Model 3:**

- *High Tier offer:* Package of Three months of services

- *Middle Tier offer:* In-person event or retreat scheduled monthly or quarterly.

- *Bite Size Offer:* Two-hour deep dive session

There are many different models to choose from. The key is to start and make sure it's priced appropriately to get you to six figures.

If you are thinking of starting a low-cost membership or an evergreen course, please wait until you have hit that Six-Figure mark. While those types of offerings can be lucrative models, they require a large audience and a working marketing and sales system in the process. Plus, you'll need FUNDS to actually support the back-end tech as well as market it well. I know there are LOTS of people out there selling the "make money in your sleep" dream, but it's just not real. Building a business takes work. It takes establishing your foundations, marketing, and sales systems and seeing that you have a service that people want before you dive into the lower-end membership/course model.

Get to six figures FIRST, and then you'll have the funds to support this as a next-level structure.

Once you have your offering firmed up, it is time to work on pricing strategy. I'll share a sample pricing strategy that I've used myself and have seen work well for the coaches and practitioners I work with. Please see these as guidelines and not hard and fast rules.

You want to price your top two offers in a way that supports both your lifestyle and time flexibility, as well as your income goals. Be mindful of your capacity for the number of clients you would need in each layer and if you have the space to actually serve them with JOY and fun. If you are undercharging for your services and pricing your packages too low, you may not have the time in your schedule that will allow you to have the lifestyle freedom you desire. So, you always want to cross-check and make sure that you are clear about not just the amount of money you want to create but the actual energy involved in delivering the program to your clients.

Your Programs and Pricing

Top Tier offer: Access to YOU. 1:1 Coaching , Masterminds

High-Mid Tier offer: 3-6 month group program

Middle Tier offer: Group program, course, short 1:1 package. Price point is under $1,000

Low Tier offer: Simple 'first thing' to get in with a customer. Assessment, deep dive session, single session Under $100 price point.

Free stuff: emails, blogs, downloads, video content, resources, PDF's, workshops, trainings and webinars

Christine Williams

Activating Heart, Soul, and Abundance
in Woman Wellness Entrepreneurs

Based on my personal experience in the coaching world working with my mentors and 100s of clients who are creating a six-figure business, an average 90-day 1:1 coaching program is $3,000. Some will charge more. But this is an average.

A high-end group coaching program can run the gamut based on the amount of 1:1 support that is included, how much access clients have to the coach, and what else is included. These can be one-year programs, group masterminds, high-end VIP days, or even weekend retreats. The key is to start someplace and get some support with this. I've seen VIP days sell for $25,000 and group weeklong retreats for $7,000. I've also seen yearlong masterminds enroll for $15,000- $80,000 and beyond.

Almost everyone struggles with the mindset around pricing their programs or offers. You'll want an experienced guide to help you with this piece so you don't undercharge or price it in the B.S zone so that you'll never offer it to anyone. (If you want in-depth training on "Mastering Your Pricing" for high-end offers, you can go here to download the free 3 day training on our book portal.

As a coach, your business model consists of TWO core main offers. You want to price them appropriately and decide how you will deliver your offers. You will also design your 90-day profit plan and your 90-day sacred self-care plan. You get to be fully sourced and nourished as you build this business, and having a sacred self-care plan is a key part of your business model and strategy. We will also talk about setting up your rhythm for success so you can flow through your days with focus and clarity instead of hustling and becoming burned out.

Your Business Model

- Top Tier Offers - $5,000 and above.

- Middle Tier offers- $500-$3,000

- Bite-size offer- $100-$500

Having TWO core main offers keeps things simple. It allows you to develop and deliver messaging around Signature Programs that you become known for and to share the ways you work with people in a way that they can understand. I see so many coaches and entrepreneurs overcomplicating this piece because they have a hard time picking just one or two of their ideas. If that's you, welcome to the world of entrepreneurship. We all have so many ideas. How do we know which one to implement? Or we dive into one and then get bored and start something new without letting the first one really gain any traction. We want to go deep here with just two instead of wide with 10 or 20.

First, get clear on your top offer. This is the offer that includes the most amount of personal 1:1 support with you. There are different ways this top offer could look. It could be a 90-day, six-month, or one-year coaching program. Or it might look like a package of 1:1 support combined with a group program. Or it could be a VIP day or a retreat. Choose what suits you, your lifestyle, and how you like to work with your clients. Inside Activate Abundance Academy, we can help you customize your pricing for your specific goals and lifestyle.

Your top-tier offer is your high-ticket offer. And you want to make sure you have one when you are building a Six-Figure business. This allows you to serve generously and really help someone create their transformation. It's a container of support for a specific time period, not just a series of 1:1 sessions. Think of this as a white glove service where you can provide your time, energy, materials, resources, and more that will help your client walk away with results. They have access to you. You are walking along the pathway with them, offering the support, structure, and accountability that is missing when trying to make changes on your own. When clients get results, they tell others, and this results in referrals and renewals. DIY courses, memberships, and one-off sessions don't do this.

I often get asked about where courses and memberships fit into your business model. Here's my answer based on experience. Courses and memberships have their place, but NOT when you are under $100,000 in revenue. You don't want to start there. Why? Because you don't yet have an audience who wants the support you provide. You don't have client results, testimonials that your process is effective, or even success in selling your offers.

Without an audience of potential clients, selling a $97-$500 course is actually a LOT harder than selling a high-ticket offer. Let's do some simple math. If you want to crate a $10,000 month and you have a high ticket offer priced at $3,000 - $5,000, you only need to sell two or three packages each month. This means that you only need to have around 15 conversations with potential clients if you have a 20% closing rate (and that's low). The method I teach has my clients enrolling 50 – 70% of their conversations.

Based on the numbers above, if you are trying to sell a $500 course, you need to sell 20 each month. This means you need to get in front of a lot more new people every month before 20 people will say yes to the offer. The same thing with a membership. A $100/month membership needs to be seen by a whole lot more people in order to sell 100 clients each month to have that $10,000 income month. And that's month after month.

So it is best to wait on courses or memberships until you are already at the $100,000- $500,000 per year of revenue in your business. You have an audience to sustain it and a budget to put into marketing it.

Your second core offer is a mid-tier offer. Think of this as a way you can still serve your ideal client but in either a shorter program or in a group. This is usually priced around $1,000 or under. These two offers help your clients get results in a way that courses and memberships do not because they are also higher in touch. In this tier, clients usually have live access to you and support to ask questions in a more intimate container than a DIY program. They usually contain a hybrid of 1:1 support and group support. Think of it this way, when clients have more accountability and support, they will implement what they learn. Less accountability and support means less implementation, which means fewer results. So, while you may THINK it's easier to sell a $100 offer, it's actually just as easy to invite someone into a container where they will get high touch, high accountability, and direct support to get them to their goals quicker.

Speed is one of the TOP things people pay for. Combine that with the other top investments, improving their health and increasing happiness, and you have offers that stand the test of time and that people are willing to invest in themselves for.

Let me share an example of how this worked for me. A couple of years ago I bought a course on copywriting. I thought it would be something that would help me speak more directly to my ideal clients. It was a perfectly good program, with a well-known influencer and copywriter. Except it was a course. So, I never opened it. There was NO accountability and no support to get my questions answered. I spent over $2,000 on something that has yet to be opened. This means I also wouldn't recommend it to anyone because I have never used it. It is not the fault of the course or the coach that sold it. It is just how our human psyche works.

Now, compare that to a program that was offered. Not a course, a program. It was a $5,000 copywriting program where I could attend live, weekly calls to answer my questions and built-in support. This prompted me to actually show up and write since I was getting direct feedback from the expert who put it all together. And guess what? It worked for me. I showed up because of the high level of support and accountability and I got results. Now, I recommend this program to everyone I know, including my clients. It helped me with speed, ideas, and ways to write copy that drew my audience in. It collapsed the timeline for me, and I had support, a system to learn how to put it on repeat, and a copywriting coach who is now the recipient of many new clients from me.

So, your TWO core offers need to be programmed, ideally with one of them being a high-end package. These two offers are your pathway to six figures.

Next, we will take a look at a high-end package and how you can make it a part of your business model.

Benefits Of Creating High-End Packages

• Your business becomes more profitable because high-end packages bring in greater income per client.

• You free your time because you don't need to work with as many people to reach your desired income goals.

• You can create greater cash flow even with a small list or a small number of contacts.

• Offering high-end packages keeps you from slipping into over delivery and burning out.

• You can focus your business on creating extraordinary results for your clients, not on selling your time, which liberates you to enjoy your business and love your life.

• You become known as one of the best at what you do.

• You keep your business simple to run, which synergistically lowers the stress of running a business.

Crafting And Pricing Your High-End Programs

In this book, I'm going to focus on a 90-day 1:1 program because that is where most coaches and practitioners start. It was also my first high ticket offer. Think about your own business. What would you want to include to make it an irresistible offer? It's important here to focus on the experience of high-touch and personal access you're providing to your clients in this container of time, not simply the number of sessions you're providing.

Each of your programs should include one item (or more) from each of these four categories:

1. Help your clients create results quickly and build momentum.

Get your clients started generating results immediately so they feel the value of their investment. This is a key moment when they are inspired and ready to take action, so help them make the most of it!

Some ways to do this are:

- Initial VIP Day (Live or Virtual)

- Group seminar/class

- Kick-start consultation

- Assessment or questionnaire

- Starter checklist

- Review of client materials (e.g., food journals, self-care plans, meal plans)

- Special reports created by outside authorities (e.g., EWG Clean 15 and Dirty Dozen list, scientific studies that support the results you help your clients with. Or even a book that supports them with additional and inspiring information.)

2. Access to Training or expert resources.

Clients love topic-specific, how-to training so look for easy ways you can deliver your expertise. Plus, during the training, you can include handouts, exercises, and activities to help them achieve their results faster.

- Done-for-You meal plans, forms, templates, checklists, etc.

- Examples of written materials you've used to achieve results

- Training/Teaching on specific topics

3.Service Delivery Methods: How will you deliver your service? And for how long? Three months, six months, one year, one day?

- Private Sessions (Coaching/Consulting)

- VIP Days (Live or Virtual)

- Group Training and/or Q&A calls

- Short emergency check-in calls/sessions

- Facebook Group

- Email

- VOXER access in a group or 1:1

- Reviews/Evaluations

- Seminars/Retreats

4.Added BONUSES

Bonuses add significant value to your program and inspire people to say "Yes!" to your offer.

- Topic-specific virtual intensives

- "Pay in full" bonuses (topic-specific bonus session/consult, webinar/video training)

- "Fast action" bonuses (additional assessments or training)

- Done-for-you materials, examples, templates, checklists

- Books/Journal

- Recordings of training and Q&A calls (for group programs)

- Seminar Ticket/Group Class Access

- Private car service to/from the airport and/or hotel

- Additional access for a guest, key employee, spouse, partner, etc.

- Featured interview to your list

Here is an example of how you can price your package. Let's base this on a $3000 program.

Full package Price $3000.00

Pay in full investment (the amount your client will pay If they pay in full" $2,500

A discount of $500 is given for payment in full.

What is your Quick Decision Savings? A quick decision saving is the amount of time you are offering your discount. This can range from 24 hours to the end of the month. What matters is that there is a time frame for this discount so that there is urgency to join you in the offer. $500

(Make it enough to inspire action! Between $300-$3000 depending on package)

Calculate your "reality check" amount

(the amount you'll actually receive)

(Full Pay Investment – Quick Decision Savings = Quick Decision Investment)

$ 2,497 - $ 500 = $ 1,997

What is the amount for a Payment Plan? $3,000

(This is often the full cost of your program because you are waiting to be paid in full.)

What is your Payment Plan Deposit and Payment Schedule

(Typically, the deposit is between 30-50% of the total.)

Deposit = $1,500

Balance = $1,500

# of payments = 3

Monthly payments = $500

Payment plan with Fast decision savings: $2,500

Deposit $1,500

Balance $1,000

# of payments = 3

Monthly payments = $334

You can try it with your own package prices here:

Price Your Package

Full Pay Investment $_____

Payment Plan Investment$_____

Deposit:

Balance:

No. of Payments:

Monthly Payment: $_____

Full Pay with Quick Decision Savings $ _____

Payment Plan with Quick Decision Savings $_____

Deposit:

Balance:

No. of Payments:

Monthly Payment: $_____

Now that you have a starting point for your premium-priced package as your high-tier offer and have your medium-tier offer, it's time to create **your 90-day profit plan.**

How many of each do you need to sell to achieve your financial goal?

Do you have the capacity to serve that many clients joyfully? Is it in alignment with your energy and resources? If Not, what needs to be adjusted? You may find you need to raise your pricing to achieve your goal and feel like you have the time and freedom you desire so you can truly be your best for yourself, your family, and your clients.

Here is an example to follow:

90-day Profit Plan:

Goal = $30,000 (this is the average $10,000 per month model)

Offer	Price	# of People Enrolled	Projected $ Made
High Tier	$5000	6 One – on – Ones	$30,000
Med Tier	$1000	10 people in a group	$10,000

Your projected income from the example above with six 1:1 clients and One group program with 10 clients is $40,000.

If you do the same each quarter this will project a yearly income of $160,000.

You can adjust as you go depending on your goals, the number of clients you wish to serve, and the number of groups you decide to run. When I ran my health coaching practice, I ran TWO groups at a time. One on Tuesday evening and one on Thursday evening. It was a six-week wellness program delivered in person and online. Out of the group, about 30% continued to work with me 1:1, which was great because that meant I didn't have to find new clients for all of my 1:1 spots. This is an important concept to remember. Give people a chance to continue to work with you. If they are in a group, invite them into 1:1 support if it's a good fit. If they are 1:1 clients, you can ask them to renew or invite them into your group. Client renewals make up about 30% of your income, so make sure to deliver excellent value and invite people to stay in your world with you.

Here's how my client Samantha created her first $10,000 month within the first three months of our program together. She had just finished her health coach certification, and we mapped out her 90-day program and priced it at $3,000. At first, she was really nervous as she had never offered a package priced at that amount. She was scared that people would not be able to afford her services or that she would be leaving people behind who really didn't have the money. She had a friend who wanted to work with her, so she gave her friend a huge discount and only charged $1,000 for the 90-day program that came with in-between support, text access, weekly 1:1 calls, and a customized health vault with resources specifically for her client. While this seemed like a great plan to her, she soon started to feel resentful. She was putting out time and energy with her friend and was answering questions and calls daily. Her friend began missing appointments and would cancel at the last minute and expect the call to be added to the end of the program. A 90-day container turned into a four-month container. She began to realize why a high-touch program like hers needed to be priced at a higher rate. The higher price ensures that the client would show up and follow through on the calls because there was actually "skin in the game.". It also protected her energy and allowed her to feel like she was being fairly compensated for her time. Not just giving away her time or advice for free whenever she answered calls or questions in between sessions. When she finally experienced this clarity, she began to value her time and her services more and attracted clients who were willing to show up, invest, and get results. She felt excited about serving them and even more confident in her pricing. The next month, she enrolled three new clients and had her first $10,000 month with clients she was excited to support and work with.

Now, let's take a closer look at capacity. We want a sustainable business. Not one where we need to work 12-hour days and on weekends. I'm a Hellz NO for that.

Design your 90-day "Sacred Self" Care Plan and Ideal Work Week.

Without You, your business won't succeed. Which means you are the golden goose. You need to take precious care of the golden goose, or she will stop laying those golden eggs. She can't lay those eggs 24/7, or she won't last very long, so you want to make sure she has plenty of rest, sunlight, time to play, nourishing food, and lots of love.

I really want you to see how important your sacred self is. How are you treating her? What do you say to her? Are you giving her the rest, sunlight, love, and nourishment she needs? Let's take a look at her non-negotiables. These are things she needs to have daily to feel fully sourced, nourished, and high vibe. When my clients start to feel overwhelmed, stressed out, or on the edge of burnout, it is most likely because they have gotten away from their non-negotiables for their own care.

Let's do that now.

First up, let's get clear on the experience you want for her.

• What does she desire in her life and business?

- How does she want it to feel?

- Who does she want to experience this with?

- Does she have kids?

- A partner?

- Does she want to travel?

- What do her days look like?

- What time does she want to get to her office?

- What feels like a good time for her to shut things down for the day?

Put those parameters in place first so that you can work your business around your life instead of life and relationships getting the leftovers.

For me, I really love having a spacious morning. I give myself a full 3 hours of time in the morning to read, pray, meditate, get a workout in, and connect over coffee with my husband.

I start my office time at 10:00 am and close it down between 5:00 pm and 6:00 pm. Anything that needs my attention after that gets attended to the next day. I don't work weekends, and I take the last week of the month off from front-facing work with my clients. This last week every month allows me to travel with my family, go away on private retreats, be visionary in my business, work on my book writing, or be creative. We all need time to unplug, renew, refresh, and be nourished. I call this Nourishing the Leader. And It's CRITICAL.

Please, hear me. This is part of your business model. It gets factored in. It's not a "nice to have." **It's a must-have.**

Here's how we do this in practical terms.

Pull out your calendar. Block out birthdays, vacations, holidays, and important times to spend with your family.

Next, block out two to three days each quarter to spend unplugged. This can be a staycation, or you can go away to someplace fun. It's time for you to dream. Be. Think. You can journal, write down your thoughts, and be the visionary in your business. You NEED this space and time to get those divine downloads that guide you through the roller coaster of entrepreneurship. You could call this a planning session or let it be a combination of planning and renewal.

Next, take a look at your month. Block out one to two days each month for FUN.

Now, write down what are the *daily non-negotiables* that keep you fully sourced, inspired, and high-vibe.

Whenever I hear/see/feel my clients getting scattered, overwhelmed, or feeling stressed out by their businesses or in their lives, this is actually the FIRST place I go with them.

Because when our foundation is wobbly, everything feels SO much harder.

Here's the good news...

THE STRUGGLE IS OPTIONAL.

Conditions to thrive or your non-negotiables are actions that create, contribute to, and sustain a nurturing environment for us to be in alignment with our souls' guidance, wisdom, and mission. A beautiful side effect is that we feel in the FLOW, magnetize our ideal client to us, create a sustainable business, and open up space for those divine downloads.

Some examples of non-negotiables are:

• Daily meditation (I do at least 10 minutes a day with my favorite app- CALM)

• Move my body 30 minutes per day

• Consume three nourishing meals per day

• Limit sugar and alcohol

• Journal daily (even if it's just one line)

• Read something inspiring and uplifting

• Get out in nature for a walk or just to sit in the sun daily

• Tidy your living and working space (this allows you to stay calm and focused)

• Block off space in your calendar for fun daily, weekly, monthly, quarterly, and yearly

• Schedule a quarterly retreat away for alone time and replenish

• Have a power down hour right before bed so you can get quality seven to nine hours of sleep per night.

• Make a list of your person's non-negotiables that create conditions to thrive and stay high vibe:

Lastly, let's create Your Contract with Yourself.

It's going to take courage and confidence to build your six-figure business. There will be times when you want to give up, shut it down, and just go get a nine-to-five JOB. But that's not really on your heart. It just happens as part of the process. We have all been there.

I NAME, accept that I'll need courage and confidence. CONFIDENCE is a CAPABILITY I'm BUILDING. For the next 12 months, This CONTRACT to myself is HOW I'm building it. The kind of courage I'll need most is:_____.

At times, things will get hard and not work. When this happens, I will double down on my commitment and have the courage to
_____ .

When in the past I would have_____.

I _____ (insert name) declare that on or before _____ (insert date one year from today), I will create the following experience of life:_____ (your signature)

Woo Hoo! You did it! This was a big chapter and full of lots of head space. Take a few moments to go outside, take a walk, and step away for a while. Then, you can come back feeling refreshed and ready to dive into the "Nurture Method.

In this chapter, you learned:

• Strategies to design your business model, pricing, and capacity.

• How to create a vision of what you want your business and lifestyle to look like and feel like in the next year.

• Ideas to create your programs and pricing.

• How to create your own signature system for the process you take your clients through.

• A profit plan for the year and the next quarter.

• The importance of a "sacred self" care plan so you stay high vibe and fully sourced as the CEO of your business.

In the next chapter, we will start putting together your plan for attracting clients into your ecosystem so they can become the paying clients in your profit plan.

Chapter 5

Steps Three, Four, and Five: The Nurture Method® (ATTRACT, NURTURE, INVITE)

"Don't be intimidated by what you don't know. That can be your greatest strength and ensure that you do things differently from everyone else." — **Sara Blakely.**

In the first step, ALIGN, we covered the importance of energetically aligning FIRST so that when we take actions, they are intentional and inspired. We also covered the importance of uncovering your ideal client and setting the foundations of a successful six-figure business with heart-centered values. Now it's time to dive into the keystone steps that you will want to hone and master. These next three steps are your anchor. Whenever my clients are feeling overwhelmed, frustrated, or just not sure what to do next, we come back here. If you are taking inspired action in each of these next three steps, your business will succeed.

In the next three steps, Attract, Nurture, and Invite, we dive into the "Nurture Method®." These steps are the cornerstones of a thriving business. Without them, you cannot build a six-figure business.

Why? Because these are the basics of your heart-centered marketing and sales system. Whenever I have felt overwhelmed, unsure of what to do next, or lacking a clear direction, I come back to these foundational steps and ask myself, what am I doing in my business to ATTRACT ideal clients into my ecosystem, NURTURE them and INVITE them to work with me.

When we look at the basics of generating revenue in your business, it comes down to three things: getting in front of your soulmate client, telling them what you do and how you can help them solve a problem, and inviting them to work with you.

The "Nurture" Method
for Heart-Centered Marketing and
Soulful Sales

The three steps are like three legs of a stool. If you are missing any one of them, the stool will fall over. Same with your business. You'll need all three steps, and here's why.

We want to attract your ideal client into your ecosystem, nurture the relationship, develop trust and belief that you can help them, and finally invite them to work with you.

Attracting the right client to you means making sure that your work and your message get in front of the people who can most benefit from your service. Just attracting people into your ecosystem isn't enough. You want the "right" people,

Think of it this way. Right now, there are three kinds of people in your world. The first are the people who I call the 'sidewalkers.'

Sidewalkers are people who don't believe they have a problem to solve. They may like FB posts and think what you do is really neat, but since they don't think they have a problem to solve, they will never be buyers. This makes up about 30% of people in your ecosystem.

Next, there are people in the slow lane. They are actively searching for a solution, but they haven't found it yet. They want their problem resolved and will invest in getting it solved. We know they are looking, so we want them to find you. These are the people we most want to get in front of and have them self-identify that they are soulmate clients. They make up about 67% of the people in your ecosystem. I'll share more about how you can get in front of them a bit.

Lastly, we have a group of people who are in the FAST lane. This group makes up about 3% of your ecosystem. And they are ready to buy from you today! They just need to be invited. They have a connection with you. You've built a "know, like, trust and rapport" with them, and they want to have you help them solve their problem.

So, if only 3% of people in your ecosystem are ready to buy, you can see why it's important to determine who are your most ideal clients that are hanging out in the slow lane looking for a solution from you. If you skip this step, you'll be nurturing and inviting people to work with you who don't see the value of your service. In turn, you'll hear lots of "No's." Or lots of "I don't have the time, or I don't have the money."

If you are attracting the right client into your ecosystem- but you lack the NURTURE step, you'll be making a premature marriage proposal. You'll be trying to take a stranger and persuade them to buy. And this can feel pushy, salesy, slimy, and so out of alignment with building a heart-centered business.

Nurturing the relationship is a process that is missing in so many systems and processes. When I went to health coaching school, I was told to just book a whole bunch of free coaching sessions and sell my 90-day program. There were no instructions on how to find the right clients and then nurture the relationship BEFORE I tried to sell the 90-day program. So, what ended up happening was that I felt out of alignment, and they did, too. And when your energy is off, potential clients feel it. I pushed through and tried to sell the way my coaches were teaching me to sell, and several things happened:

• People didn't show up for the free coaching call (they had no skin in the game to motivate them)

• I was in the energy of scarcity and felt the need to convince my network to buy from me, which made my sales pitch NOT heart-centered

• Potential clients felt pushed or rushed into making a decision and so the invitation to work with me ended in a no.

So, really take some time and nurture the relationship with potential clients so it doesn't feel like a premature marriage proposal. People want to feel seen, heard, and supported before they trust you and feel a connection to you. Think of this as putting money in the bank of reciprocity. I like to think of it like the "Generosity Game." The more value I put out in the world, the more trust and belief people have in my ability to support them. And the only people that buy are the ones that have trust and belief in you and your offers. So, share your best stuff. Lead with value. Share free resources that help your potential clients create wins.

After you have nurtured your potential clients, you move to the INVITE step. If you lack the invite step, you have your ideal client, and you've done a really great job connecting and building trust, but if you don't invite them to take the next to work with you, you're abandoning them on pain island. I see lots of wellness coaches and holistic practitioners getting stuck at this step. They serve and nurture all day- but never invite their potential clients to the party. And people WANT to be invited. Remember, they are looking for a solution. If you don't invite them to work with you, they will work with someone else.

One of my coaches and mentors, Fabienne Frederickson, explains it like this. Imagine you have a party at your house, and you've promised the most amazing brownies. Everyone has heard about them, can smell them baking and they are just waiting to taste them. But you never bring them out of the kitchen. You never offer your guests a brownie so they can enjoy the chocolatey goodness. How rude. They walk away from the party disappointed and wonder why you invited them to the party and told them about the brownies if you weren't going to share them.

That is what happens when you attract and nurture - but don't invite. And the real cause of this fear around inviting has nothing to do with the potential client. It has everything to do with you. I'll dive into this in the Invite chapter, and we'll pull back the curtains on what is really going on and how to solve it.

In this chapter, you learned:

• The importance of having a complete Nurture Method, composed of ATTRACT, NURTURE, and INVITE, and why you need all three in order to build a prosperous holistic business.

• Why it is important to attract the right clients into your ecosystem.

• The importance of nurturing relationships BEFORE asking people to buy.

• When to invite clients to work with you and why you can't build a business without making an invitation.

Now that you can see how important each step is in the process and how you can't build a prosperous business without ALL of them, the next three chapters will cover each one individually.

Let's dive into client ATTRACTION.

Chapter 6
Step Three: Attract

"Success isn't about how much money you make; it's about the difference you make in people's lives." – **Michelle Obama.**

Notice that the word is ATTRACT. It's not chase. It's not drag. It's not harass. Attraction is based on pull marketing. Pulling or attracting your ideal client to you by being visible and sharing value that solves a piece of their problem. It's based on giving value FIRST and cultivating a relationship before you ask them to buy. There is no need to manipulate, convince, or drag anyone across the finish line because you are simply being of service.

Picture this. You have this beautiful mansion. Inside there are different rooms used for different purposes. There is a kitchen to host intimate gatherings and be more focused on conversations and a fireside chat. Then, there is the backyard pool area, which is great for hosting a large party where people can gather and connect in a group. Upstairs is the penthouse with a gorgeous view and a luxurious space where champagne and chocolate-covered strawberries are served.

Now, imagine a sidewalk running in front of the house and a pathway leading from the sidewalk to the mansion. Before you actually walk into the mansion there is a front porch with a comforting porch swing. Along the pathway are a few benches that lead to this porch.

This pathway is what attracts people who are walking along the sidewalk. They are just walking along and see a beautiful and welcoming opportunity to come sit. So, they turn off the sidewalk, head down the path, and stop at one of the benches. The benches are pieces of value you are sharing with them. They are your high-value opt-ins or lead magnets that solve a problem your potential client is having now. You have caught their eye and attention, and they have turned on their own accord to check out the bench. To come, have a seat, and experience what is there. Once they sit for a while, they may move onto another bench (another free offer, masterclass, workshop, or assessment). At some point, they may actually join you up on the front porch swing, where you can have a conversation about the various rooms in your mansion and which they might like to explore. This is pull marketing. You are attracting them from the sidewalk with a service, value, or way to begin a relationship with a potential client. Once they turn from the sidewalk to the pathway, they have moved from stranger to viewer. They have pre-qualified themselves because they have shown interest in having what you are sharing. They are raising their hand, telling you they want what you have to offer. I call this self-identification. Your potential clients self-identify by asking for your free value. The marketing term is a lead magnet, but I find that term feels cold and impersonal. I see people on my pathway as people and relationships, not just leads.

Once they are here, you now have an opportunity to step from the front porch and meet them at a bench. Have a conversation, help them create a quick win or an epiphany, and then invite them to join you on the front porch. Once they sit on the porch, they have moved from a viewer to a potential client. They are even more interested in seeing more of the grounds, gardens, or even the inside of the mansion, and you can explain what rooms you have inside the mansion and help them decide which one may be the best fit for them. Are they looking for a luxurious penthouse experience? Maybe they want to be part of a group experience and hang out by the pool? OR maybe they just want a relaxed chat by the kitchen fireside. These rooms represent your offers. And they each meet a need for your potential client based on what experience THEY desire, not what you are pushing to sell. And doesn't that feel just so freeing? There is no pressure to go GET a client from the sidewalk and drag them into your mansion to buy. No objections to overcome. No sales-y or slimy tactics. Just a genuine desire to share value, create a relationship, and invite them to take the natural next step to work with you if they desire.

Let's talk about your benches. How are you being visible to who you can help? Where are you being visible? What value are you sharing?

One of the first things you need to do to help you attract more clients and get your practice full is to make certain that you actually create time for marketing. Don't let the word marketing scare you. It's simply sharing your message and mission on how you can help people.

There are many ways to do this. **You can find my free handout on 30 ways to attract your ideal client in the 'book portal here.' I even share 21 high-converting lead magnet ideas to help you with your own.**

I'd like to share a few ways that I attract clients into my world and the benches that I offer. See if one of them feels like something you'd like to try.

Client Attraction Wheel

50% of your time in your business should be devoted to client attraction

Stages, networking groups, podcasts, summits — Speaking

Free offers

Nurture Events — Online or in person events, talks masterclasses etc.

Content, Reels, FB groups, Video — Social Media

leads & paying clients

Email — Newsletters, stay in touch, personal blog, value

Print or digital magazine, other peoples blogs, content sites — Articles

Networking + Associations

referrals and collab's — Joint ventures, affiliates, clients, collaborations, joint workshops

Networking groups local and online

Shine Abundance Now.com. Shine Wellness LLC

1.**Share a valuable freebie.** People want an experience of what you have to offer them before they buy. They want to see if what you are sharing is really for them. So, create something that is HIGH value to them in exchange for their email. High value means that it's simple for them to consume. They REALLY want it because it solves a problem. They can reuse it over and over again. This is key, because it keeps you top of mind for them and establishes you as an expert in your field/niche and will help you create that trust that is so necessary before they buy.

Some examples that fall into this category that work really well are:

- Checklists

- Templates

- Assessments

- Quizzes

- Workshops

- Lunch and learns

- Talks

- Free tickets to your event

- Speaking on stages

- Speaking on podcasts

- Being a guest expert in someone's program

- Collaborating with others and doing free training in their community

When we offer something for free, we want to keep in mind the MOTIVATORS for people. Let's refer to a list of the top 10 reasons, motivators, results, or benefits that make people buy, according to Jim Edwards and David Garfinkel in their eBook entitled "eBook Secrets Exposed" you can find it at www.EbookSecretsExposed.com:

Here, according to them, are the most powerful motivators:

1.   Make money

2. Save money

3. Save time

4. Avoid effort

5. Get more comfort

6. Achieve greater cleanliness

7. Attain better health

8. Escape physical pain

9. Gain praise

10. Be popular

So, when creating the high-value freebie you want to share (one of your benches) with potential clients, make sure it solves a problem that falls into one of these categories and that it is also relevant and congruent with how you help people solve their problem. Make sure this is an actual problem that they have NOW. The online space has changed, and people are more discerning and cautious. Their BS meter is on alert. They don't want to waste time and will not respond if they don't see that what you have to offer will actually solve the current problem they are facing.

If you are not sure what your ideal clients struggle with, you'll want to take some time and do some market research. ASK your potential clients what keeps them up at night? What are they googling an answer for? What words are they using? Many coaches and practitioners get stuck here because they keep their coaching hats on instead of taking time to step into their ideal clients' shoes. For example, no one is waking up wanting to join a 14-day liver cleanse. Maybe you think that's what they need, but that's not going to have people raising their hands to join you. They are asking for chocolate, and you are leading with broccoli. You need to speak chocolate FIRST, and then you can give them the broccoli that they need once they are working with you.

Here's an example that may help. My client, Rose, is a Functional Nutritional Therapy Practitioner. Based on her training, she knows that health starts in the digestive system. that being out of balance digestively leads to many other problems and diseases, and that high amounts of sugar affect the microbiome and, in turn, create low energy. But her potential clients don't know that. All they know is that they are feeling tired, have low energy, and suffer from uncontrollable cravings. What they want is more energy. Not a sugar detox. Do they need to cut down on their sugar? Most likely. But that's not what they are asking for. They are asking for more energy. So. Rose created a freebie with 10 ways to have more energy during the day. This freebie is solving the problem her potential clients are having. She can always talk about the importance of lowering sugar, eating a healthy whole-food diet, getting plenty of rest, etc. But if she leads with "who wants to give up sugar for 30 days, she won't get a lot of hands being raised.

2.**Live Informational sessions.** If you attract most of your potential clients online, one way to pull clients into your eco-system is to share value in a weekly Facebook live. This is one of my favorite ways to pull clients into my eco-system, and I host the live inside my private Facebook Group. The Facebook group is FREE to be a part of, but it's ONLY for my ideal clients, my strategic partners, or my champions. If they are not one of those, they are not a good fit for the group because they won't receive value. And, if they don't receive value, they won't engage in the group, which means they are not a good fit for the way I can help them.

Facebook is my all-time favorite social media platform. It's free, easy to leverage and scale, and has my ideal client hanging out there. According to the Pew research center, Facebook is one of the most widely used online platforms in the U.S. among adults.

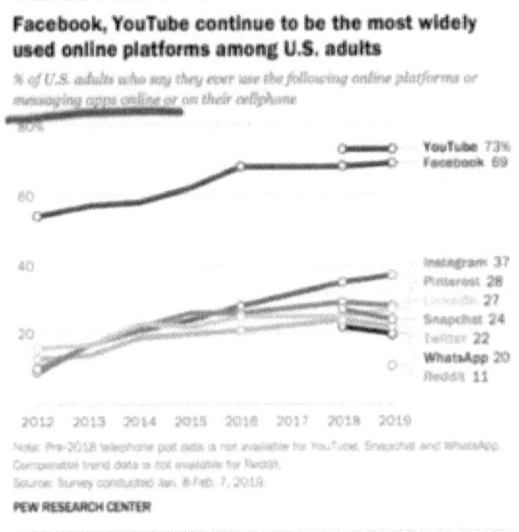

Facebook, YouTube continue to be the most widely used online platforms among U.S. adults

% of U.S. adults who say they ever use the following online platforms or messaging apps online or on their cellphone

YouTube 73%
Facebook 69
Instagram 37
Pinterest 28
LinkedIn 27
Snapchat 24
Twitter 22
WhatsApp 20
Reddit 11

2012 2013 2014 2015 2016 2017 2018 2019

Note: Pre-2018 telephone poll data is not available for YouTube, Snapchat and WhatsApp. Comparable trend data is not available for Reddit.
Source: Survey conducted Jan. 8-Feb. 7, 2019.

PEW RESEARCH CENTER

The other cool thing about Facebook is that it is a robust platform. It's not just about your Facebook profile. There are actually multiple ways to use it to create visibility and attract your ideal into your ecosystem.

I have found that Facebook groups are one of the best ways to be visible in front of my most ideal clients. It allows me to cultivate an online community of engaged, soulmate potential clients. And Facebook promotes their Facebook groups. They WANT people to stay on their platform and promote groups.

I've even seen T.V. ads on Facebook promoting groups as a way to connect with others.

You can also utilize Facebook Reels and Facebook stories for your personal profile, business pages, event Pages, messenger, marketplace, Facebook lives, chats, and ways to share your videos, photos, and freebies. All in ONE place.

If you are a coach or holistic practitioner and are not yet using Facebook, I encourage you to take another look. There are benefits to sticking with just ONE platform. It allows you to simplify your focus, your attention, and your time on where your ideal client is. Instead of trying to be on ALL the platforms that can split your time and overwhelm, stick to one and become an expert on how to use it to get in front of your soulmate client to grow your business...

I see way too many mistakes with new entrepreneurs trying to be in all the places, and it just leads to procrastination and never getting anything going well. Dig your well deep first before you go wide.

There is a time and a place to get more visible on other platforms, but wait until you've hit six figures first.

3. **Email List.** The best practice for building your business and attracting soulmate clients is to have an email list and a presence online. An email list is what you own. A social media presence is something you rent. Social media sites own their own platforms and can close them down at any time, so having the

additional email marketing platform ensures that you can still serve and communicate with your ideal clients.

There are lots of email marketing platforms to choose from. Mail Chimp, Mailer Lite, Constant Contact, Flo Desk, and ConvertKit. I personally love ConvertKit if you're just starting out. It allows you to create landing pages with ease to share your freebies, gather emails, and send out valuable information to the people who most want it.

Since I mentioned Facebook groups earlier as a way to ATTRACT your audience, I want to share a bit more detail. You know who your ideal client from the ALIGN chapter is; now, you want to give your people a place to land online. A place for them to have a sense of belonging. You'll want to pick a name for your Facebook group based on the result you want them to achieve and who your ideal client is. My Facebook group is called Holistic Business Success: Soulful Strategies For 6-Figures and Beyond. (You can check it out here: https://www.facebook.com/groups/2108975265997592)

It tells you the result my ideal clients want: to build a six-figure business. And who it's for: people who want to grow a holistic business in a soulful way. Now, when people see the title or do a search, they will know if it's for them. It's only going to be attractive to the people who I can best serve.

Once you have created your group, you'll want to start adding some value. Within a Facebook group, there is a files section where you can upload PDFs, infographics, and material that helps your audience create some connection to you and shows how you can help them. If you have had some clients, you can add a video or written testimonials so people can see the results they can expect to get by working with you. If you add a free checklist or handout in the files, you can invite people to join your group, and as a thank you they receive the freebie. It's easy to do this by sharing a post on your personal Facebook page with a colored background asking, "Who are my people who would like my free resource on…" Then, the ones that reply, you can reach out to directly in messenger and say, "Thanks for commenting on my post about the x,y, z resource. It's located inside my free Facebook group. Can I share the link with you?" When they reply YES, simply share the URL link of your Facebook group and then tag them in the post where the resource is located. You now have attracted someone into your ecosystem.

4.**Podcasts, Summits, YouTube**. These are virtual ways you can leverage other people's audiences by being featured as a guest. Being a guest expert on someone's podcast, as part of a summit or on someone's YouTube Channel will introduce you to people outside of your network that are in the slow lane. Most channels and summits allow you to share your freebie link, so you will be attracting the right client who is interested in your free resource. This allows you to receive their email address and serve them even more by nurturing them with more value. (I'll share more about this in the next chapter) Being on these platforms online helps to create visibility in multiple places, establishes you as an expert and helps build your authority in your niche and field.

So far, we have talked about online marketing, but you can also use 'pull marketing' in person. For many years, before I took my business online, I marketed my health coaching services in multiple ways. The way I chose to attract my ideal client was to give free talks and collaborate with referral partners. I would collaborate with a doctor or holistic health practitioner and offer to do a free talk to their clients or patients. My talk was always based on helping them learn some ways they could create a win or an epiphany on their health journey. During my talk, I would share how they could have my support in implementing some of the tips I shared if they desired. My talks gave people the *What* and the *Why* of better health. The HOW they would get when they decided to work with me. It was a fun way for me to teach, give value, and help people see how they could overcome a health challenge. There was no pressure. And I always walked away with at least one new private client after every talk. If the offer was to join me in a group program, several people from each talk would ask for a conversation to explore if it would be a good fit for them.

Talks do several things well to attract the RIGHT clients to us. First, they prequalify the client before they show up. No one is going to come to a talk if they are not interested in the topic. So, the fact that they showed up to hear you speak and share value means they are already interested in the way you may be able to help them.

Second, it establishes you as an expert. Attendees of scheduled events are coming to hear information they wish to learn. And you are the expert that is leading the conversation.

Third, it leverages other people's audiences and takes all the heavy lifting off of you to be visible. The individual hosting the event is sharing you with their clients. This means you'll be visible to people who are not part of your normal warm circle. But once you meet them, now they are part of your ecosystem and you can continue to nurture them, which we will talk about in the next chapter. There is also a transfer of trust that happens. People who trust their doctor, chiropractor, or practitioner will also be more open to trusting you because you came recommended. How many times have you tried a new restaurant because a friend told you about it? Or a clothing store or product? I've asked my friends for recommendations and trusted the names they gave me because I trust my friends. The majority of the heavy lifting to create trust and visibility has already occurred before the talk even takes place. How cool is that?

Some other places to give talks are conventions, local networking groups, meet-ups, women's groups, church groups, small business associations, and even places like workout facilities. I have given talks at a local Pure Barre Studio, 9-Round Studio, Yoga Studio, Massage Therapy practice, Acupuncture Office, Wellness Center, Integrative Doctor's Office, Chiropractors office, and Curves for Women. The key is to go where your ideal client is. Who are some of the other practitioners she/he goes to that is a complimentary value to them on their health or wellness journey? Some of my clients have given talks at wineries, health food stores, Clean Juice, and ladies' night out parties. The possibilities are abundant.

Your talk can also be given at someone's live event. We call these stages. For example, my coach, Sara Connell, runs an in-person live event every spring and every fall. She attracts coaches and thought leaders who want to write a book and help get their work into the world. My ideal client of a coach or wellness entrepreneur is in her audience, so it makes sense for me to be a speaker and share some of my helpful tips with her audience. This allows me to share value and gift a free resource that speaks to my ideal client.

5. **Print and digital magazines and blogs**. Another way to attract your client is by being featured in a magazine (both print and digital) or on someone's blog. This is another way to tap into collaborations with someone who can introduce you to their audience so you can gain visibility and share your resources.

Your next step is to brainstorm how you want to ATTRACT your ideal client into your ecosystem. First, decide if you want to attract them online or in person. Then decide on what you want to share that is of value to your audience and that solves the problem that they have. A free handout or checklist can also work really well for your in-person talks. You can pass around a clipboard with places for people to include their names and email addresses so you know where to send the free handout. This allows you to build your email list and continue to deliver value to them even after the talk. Take a look at my free checklist on *55 Places to Find Your Ideal Client* and *22 Highly Converting Freebies* to give you ideas. You can access that HERE. https://learn.shineabundancenow.com/freebies-that-convert

Pick one online platform to share your freebie and one in-person place to share value. Don't try to start with them all. It will lead to overwhelm and burnout. For now, just pick two. As you get more comfortable, you can add more ways to become omnipresent. And don't forget to repurpose your content. A video can be transcribed into an article, blog, or social media post. A blog can be shared on someone else's blog or newsletter, as an article, or even as a freebie. The key is to find where your ideal client is, and share your resources there. Repurpose as much as possible so you don't feel like you're on the content creation hamster wheel, and stay consistent.

I want to share how my client Betty did this. When she first started her coaching practice, she felt like she had to be on ALL the platforms. She had an Instagram account, Pinterest, LinkedIn and Facebook. She was trying to be consistent in all these places but was failing miserably. She felt like all she did was spend time online behind her computer. She felt frustrated because she was posting, but no one was engaging with her content. Betty was using the old, outdated way of posting. She was posting a tip, then dm-ing anyone who liked it and trying to give them a free one-hour discovery session to sell her program. She told me she couldn't make any sales and wanted to give up on her dream of having a profitable coaching practice. We decided to work together to make some changes. First, she scaled back to the ONE online platform where she knew her clients were spending time. That turned out to be Facebook. She started a Facebook community and made a plan to not just share tips but to share actual value with her potential clients. Pretty soon people were asking her for the resources she was sharing

142

and messaging her for more information on how they could have her support. She started feeling excited about her business again and worked only on building her Facebook community and sharing a lead magnet to build her email list. In three months she had three new high-tier clients and was feeling happy and fulfilled, and she had time and space to spend time offline doing more hiking with her family. Betty's community continued to grow, and after just one year, she had her highest month ever, bringing in over $12,000 cash into her business. Simplification is what created momentum for her. Focusing on relationships over transactions and leading with value, generosity, and service made her LOVE the way she was marketing and sharing her message.

In this chapter, you learned:

• How someone moves along the client pathway from a stranger to a buyer.

• Where to start to attract your ideal client into your ecosystem.

• Your client attraction wheel with various ways (benches) to bring someone into your ecosystem.

• The importance of leading with value and generosity for the win.

In the next chapter, NURTURE, I'll share what to do with your new potential clients to move them along the client attraction pathway from the potential client to the buyer. All with permission-based, pull marketing that is heart-centered and full of value.

Chapter 7
Step 4:NURTURE

"Passion is energy. Feel the power that comes from focusing on what excites you." – **Oprah Winfrey**

Whoo Hoo. Here we are with some potential clients in your ecosystem. You've attracted them with value and now what do you do with them? It's time to Nurture those relationships and give them a personal touch to help them learn more about how you can support them in creating the transformation they desire.

All Nurture Events are designed to give people an experience of you and see how you can help them along the pathway from where they are now to the transformation they desire to have. Live events are just a method to meet with people in person and locally and share what you do and how you serve them. Online events can extend to a global population. Which means you can serve more people in a virtual event. I've had people from Africa, Ireland, Italy, Australia, Canada, and all over the USA, but running a virtual event from my office in North Carolina.

Many certification programs completely pass over this critical piece of running a business. I know. I spent tens of thousands of dollars on a mastery-level program that just taught people to book discovery sessions to create sales. While I love chatting with potential clients, the problem with just booking discovery calls is that there is no nurturing or pre-qualifying prior to the call. Trying to turn a stranger into a buyer is like a premature marriage proposal. Not only is that not effective, but it's an outdated approach that only works with your HOT leads who already have an experience of "know like, trust" with you. We need this in between step to Nurture the new people in our ecosystem and guide them along the pathway to take the natural next step with us. Not the premature sales pitch.

One of the most effective ways to Nurture is with what I call "Nurture Events." These events can be online or in person, and they are a critical component of growing "know like, trust" with your audience. Nobody will buy or invest in someone they don't trust. They also won't buy if they don't have a sense of certainty that you can support them in their end result. Nurture Events do both. They build trust and they also build belief that you are the best person to help them.

I'm going to break down Nurture Events into two categories. **In-person nurture events** and **online nurture events.** Both work. It all depends on your business and what feels the most exciting and aligned for you, as well as your budget for running your event.

In-Person Nurture Events

In-person nurture events can take many forms. From a simple "lunch and learn" or "fireside chat" to a multi-day live event or conference. They can also be paid or free, depending on the outcome you desire.

You may have attended a few of these events yourself.

See if you recognize any below and put a star next to the ones that might feel exciting for you.

• Corporate Lunch and Learns that a corporation or business hosts

• Talks that you host yourself at a space you rent

• Hosted talks that a collaboration partner hosts for you

• Speaking on someone's live stage at a conference as a keynote speaker

• Putting on your own in-person one-day event at a location you reserve

• Putting on your own in-person multiple-day event

• Creating a meet-up group with monthly meetings and sharing your tips

• Hosting retreats

The key to all of these is that YOU are the person they are coming to see. They are coming to hear you talk and share your brilliance and tips. You will also be sharing ways people can continue to have your support after the event, so you will want to have an offer that you will be guiding them to.

Christine Williams

One of my favorite in-person Nurture Events that I did while growing my wellness business was a one-hour to 90-minute talk that a collaboration partner hosted for me. I asked a friend of mine who was a chiropractor if I could give a free health talk to his patients. I knew that what I had to share would help his patients in a way that was complementary to the care he was giving them. This type of Nurture Event actually helped with the Attract step of bringing people into my world *and* the Nurture steps of teaching them something of value they wanted to learn, and building "know, like, trust" quickly because we were in a face-to-face experience. It also included the Invite step of giving them a natural next step to take after the talk was complete.

The beauty of why this works so well is that your collaboration partner gets the people to the event for you. They invite the people from their practice or audience. And when they do that, a natural transfer of trust occurs. Meaning, that if your collaboration partner has a community that values and trusts them, then their community will also value and trust their recommendation of you. This takes all the heavy lifting off of your shoulders of getting people there and reduces any expenses for putting on the event.

For example, when I was growing my health coaching practice, I collaborated with doctors, acupuncturists, chiropractors, massage therapists, and integrative doctors. I would meet with them first and learn more about what their business mission was and how I could help them with that mission. Since they were all focused on helping others live and

148

lead happier, healthier lives, our missions matched. So when I offered to come to their office and give a free health talk, they were more than willing to share it with their clients. This allowed me to get in front of ideal clients who were focused on creating better health for themselves, which was my ideal client. However, I helped them in a different way than my collaboration partner. I became the bridge between the doctor or healthcare professional and the client who needed more hand-holding. I was able to do the hand-holding and develop with them a system to know what steps to take to actually develop long-term healthy lifestyle habits, which was something that the doctors didn't have time to focus on.

I teach more about this inside my free training "Collaborations Made Easy." You can access that free training inside the portal here.

I created a signature talk entitled "Get Your Spark Back" for these gatherings that I used over and over again. The simplicity of this method is that it allows you to hone in and master one main talk. It's repeatable and you can always change the title of the talk to meet the needs of your audience rather than creating a whole new talk. No matter what type of in-person event you're speaking at, your signature talk helps you deliver value to the audience and speaks to the problems they want to be solved and how you are the person to help them get the solution.

During your signature talk, you are going to share the signature system that we created in the Design step. This allows you to continue to bring the focus back to what makes you unique and why people will see you as the best person to help them. Sharing your signature system allows them to experience your process and the pathway to help them create the transformation they want.

While the scope of this book doesn't allow time to actually teach you how to write your own talk or how to create all the assets of planning your event, I do teach that inside my program Activate Abundance® Academy and give my clients several of my personal talks that they can adjust or use as inspiration to make their own. In the paragraphs below, I'll share some tips to make your talk an effective means of inviting clients to work with you and converting potential clients to buyers.

Think of your Nurture Event as another layer of an onion. The first layer is to pique their interest with the event title. This will attract the clients to you who are the best fit for how you help people. Remember in the last chapter where I shared the difference between the language of chocolate and broccoli? We want the talk title to be in the language of chocolate. Something your potential clients want and desire. Since my ideal clients are women who are feeling tired, burned out, and lacking vitality in their lives, my talk "Get your Spark Back" spoke directly to the result they wanted. It was attractive to them, and they could see that when they came to listen to my talk, they would walk away with new ideas on how they could feel energized and excited about life again. Then, during the actual talk, I gave them an EXPERIENCE. I walked them through my proprietary steps so they had a clear understanding of how I could help them solve their problem. Many of my potential clients were struggling with an all-or-nothing mentality. When they stayed on a diet, they felt like they were succeeding, but when they fell off their plan, they binged and threw in the towel and told themselves they would just start again on Monday. I walked them through the power of letting go of this perfectionist view of what they thought their health plan should be like. Instead of an all-or-nothing mentality, we talked about the power of small, manageable steps, letting each meal be a new choice, giving themselves grace and compassion, and celebrating tiny wins. They walked away feeling seen and heard, and they created some quick wins and epiphanies on what they could implement to start feeling healthier and happier right away. This built trust with me quickly, so they naturally wanted to learn how to take the next step and have my support in implementing what I was teaching them.

By the end of the event, your potential clients will either want to stay in your world and learn more, decide that your method is not right for them, or join you in your offer. All three are a win. If they stay in your world, they are in the slow lane and just need a bit more nurturing before they decide to invest in your support. If they decide your method is not right for them, they are self-selecting that they are not your person. And if they join you in your offer, you just created a buyer and generated income with a client who needs you and the support you provide.

If you decide that you want to put on your own event rather than working with a collaboration partner, it will require more planning and a promotional period to get people to attend. There is a lot more work that goes into it, the biggest of which is securing a location and paying for any event space and the other expenses that go with it.

If you are just starting your business, I suggest getting your feet wet with in-person events by taking the one-hour talk route with a collaboration partner. I mentioned how I did that above and you can access my free training on getting booked with collaboration partners in the portal. Get that working well first; then, once you know this talk converts well, and once you have an idea of what resonates and doesn't with your audience, you can create a larger event that you host on your own.

Here's what you will need to put on your one-hour talk with a collaboration partner.

- Your signature system/ framework

- A talk that takes people through your system. Limit it to four to six steps or tips. (You can grab my free talk outline in the online portal)

- A collaboration partner to host the event for you (you can check out my free workshop called "Collaborations Made Easy" in the portal to help you learn how to create perfect collaboration partners)

- A signup sheet so you can collect names and email addresses at the event

- A free handout of the steps that you give them when they give you their name and email address

- A Facebook group where you will guide them after your talk. (You can create a simple QR code or link on your handout to do this as well as mention it in your talk. I'll talk more about Facebook groups later in this chapter.)

- A separate sign-up sheet where they can book a free 30-minute clarity call with you to help them with the next steps of solving their problem. (You can also have a QR code that will take them to your online booking system)

- An offer. How do you work with clients? What program or offer will you share with those people who are ready to say YES to having your support?

- A follow-up email after the talk.

There are five stages to a successful Nurture Event that you do in person vs online.

- **Plan your event -** Have your talk, talk title, and flier ready to go so you can share it with potential collaboration partners/spaces.

- **Promote your event- Once you have a date agreed upon with your host,** provide an email copy, as well as flyers or cards that they can use to promote the event. (You want to make it easy for them.) You will also want to look at where else you can promote the event. Some online sites to look into are Eventbrite and Meet-up. They allow you to advertise your in-person event. Other ideas to consider: Is there a local networking group you can share it with? Give yourself three to four weeks to promote your event to get enough people there.

- **Run your event-** Give your talk and invite your audience to the offer between steps four and six. You don't want to wait until the end of the talk as people are expecting a pitch. Instead, recap the first four steps you shared and then open to your offer. Be sure to focus on the results they get by taking you up on your offer. Then, share the last few steps. At the end of your talk, remind them of the offer and say thank you. Remind them of any pricing bonuses or extra value they get by taking action BEFORE the event ends.

- **Follow-up:** Within the three days following the event, send an email to everyone who attended, along with a thank you card to the host (your collaborative partner). In the email, tell the attendees how you know them and what they are experiencing, and thank them for coming to the event. Share your link to the landing page for the offer or a link to book a clarity call with you. This reminds them that the door is open to invite them to connect with you again. You can also invite them again to your Facebook community so you can continue to nurture the relationship. Remember, this is where you are coming from a place of service and generosity. You are building relationships with people who are not yet ready to work with you. There needs to be a transfer of trust before they can buy, and that requires you to continue delivering value and helping them see that you are the one they want to work with to attain their results.

• **Debrief-** The intention of the debrief is to gather information to help you run the event again, but even better next time. Ask yourself three questions.

a. What went well?

b. What was MEH that you would like to improve?

c. What will you not want to do again?

Some Secrets to a Successful Talk

• **Keep Everything Ready-to-Go-** *This prevents last-minute scattered preparations that can throw you off.*

• **Show up to the location 30 minutes early** *to get grounded and familiar with your surroundings and be calm. Visualize the talk going smoothly and people enjoying it, being engaged, and wanting to know more.*

- **Plan Your Signature Outfit-** *This makes you feel confident and ready to receive bookings and saves a lot of time and energy. Wear colors you feel good in, and an outfit you feel represents you and your brand.*

- **Eat For Energy-** *Bring some water and a simple snack, so you have the energy to deliver powerfully.*

Once you've mastered the one-hour talk as a Nurture Event, it's time to look at larger in-person events.

- *Retreats-* These require more planning and an upfront investment to secure a location. You will want to promote the event four to six months prior so that you have ample time to fill the spots. These can be as simple as a one-day retreat or a multi-day retreat. The key is to give people an amazing experience so that they want to continue to work with you. What I love about retreats is that you have more time to spend with people and really get to know them. They are usually more intimate and provide exceptional value. Be sure to decide what offer you will be inviting people to next.

o Secrets to Successful Retreats

▪ Plan ahead of time and decide who is the best fit to be an attendee at the retreat.

▪ Have a theme. This provides structure to what you want your guests to experience.

- Decide if you want to provide food and snacks. If so, see if the venue provides them or if you want your guests to be on their own for meals.

- Make sure the venue is on brand with the experience you want your community to have. (ex. If your people like being in nature- don't keep them cooped up in a conference room.)

- Offer some welcome gifts or swag they can take home to remember you and the experience.

- Decide if this is a paid or free retreat. You could also deliver the experience for free and have them pay for their meals and accommodations. There are multiple options here.

- *Conference Events-* Conference events are not for the beginner. These require the most amount of planning. If you have not yet run a conference, consider investing in an event planner to help you. You will want to decide on the location, the venue, the food, the room setup, guest rooms if needed, and the total upfront investment. This is a more advanced event and comes with the biggest amount of financial risk and potential gain. I know coaches who have brought in $500,000 in revenue from just one three-day event. Just like all events, you will want to know what offer you will be inviting them to. This type of event is about getting lots of your ideal clients there. It is usually, but not always, smart to make this a low-cost attendance event to encourage registrations. The benefit is having more people come to have an experience and to pitch your offer, therefore recouping your expenses and generating revenue. You will want to have your talk dialed in for each day and have presented the information previously so you know it resonates well with your audience and converts to paying clients.

Now, let's dive into how to do this online and virtually.

• *Online Virtual Events:* Just like in-person talks, these will be focused on teaching your audience your signature system or method. They can be one-hour workshops, several-hour workshops, multiple-day masterclasses or challenges, or even joint events with collaboration partners. There are so many versions of how you can do these, but I'll stick with sharing what I do and what I teach my clients inside my programs.

• My favorite virtual nurture events are *LIVE online three to five-day masterclasses*. I learned this method from my former coach, Megan Huber, and then from the live launch queen herself, Kelly Roach. These virtual events have helped me generate over Two Million dollars in my business. Five days seems to be the sweet spot. It gives just enough time to create a relationship with your audience without losing them at the end. Each day's presentation is about 45-60 minutes long and follows your signature system. It's a good idea to have the same time each day to keep continuity. You could also offer a morning option and an evening option if you are serving people in multiple time zones. I prefer to do these live one time and then offer replays to those who registered for the event. The reason why these are multiple-day events is that in today's market, it takes up to 11 pieces of value to build trust. And up to 20-40 touches before someone becomes a buyer. That means that they will be in your ecosystem anywhere from six to twelve months before they say YES to buy and may even come to two, three, or four of your online events. Gone are the days when people would opt-in to watch a webinar recording and, after the recording, buy your program. People have gotten burned by programs in the past, and they are much more discerning. So, it's taking longer for them to buy once they enter your ecosystem. That means you need to be able to deliver value in a time frame where you can give them those 11 pieces of value and build that trust. It's so much easier to do that in a multiple-day event. It shortens the time they need to feel connected to you. It allows them to see the value of what you are teaching them, connect with them live, and cultivate a connection during and after the event.

• There are a lot of moving pieces to this type of event, but it's actually a really fun, low-tech, and low-expense. All you need is a Facebook group and or a Zoom room and a few assets that I'll share next. You can access my "Cheat Sheet" for virtual nurture events in the online portal.

Here are the assets you'll need:

• **An email marketing system.** There are lots out there. The most common are MailChimp, Constant Contact, Convertkit, FloDesk, or larger systems like Kajabi, Kartra Etc.

• **A registration page for the event.** This is also called a landing page or opt-in page and is created through your email marketing system. (I use ConvertKit) This allows you to collect the names and email addresses of the people who are registered for your event and allows you to send the other assets to make the experience valuable to them.

• **A Workbook/Action Guide/Playbook.** Workbooks guide people through your process and add value to your talk. This gives people an additional incentive to register for the event. It is a high-value handout that people can refer to during the event (and even after if they so choose) that has your name and website on it. This keeps you front of mind and is also an easy way to deliver the material. You can create this inside Canva or on your computer and download it as a PDF. Your email provider will be able to deliver this workbook to them once they register for the event.

• **A Zoom Account.** This allows you to invite them directly to your private Zoom room and actually see them. I find it so much more fun to actually see your audience and be able to respond to them directly than just speaking to air on a recording. It gives a more intimate experience and feels like a two-way connection with your attendees.

• **A Facebook Group-** This can be either a pop-up group or your private Facebook group community. Facebook groups are critical in bringing people together in one central place that gives people a sense of community and connection while they are learning.

• **Emails to promote the event to your email list so they see the value of why they want to attend.**

- **Social media posts and catchy graphics to draw people to the event.**

- **(Optional) People to share the event with you.** These can be collaboration partners, affiliates, friends, or clients. They can share your emails or social posts with their communities.

- **Emails to send after the event with your offer**

There are 5 stages to running a successful virtual Nurture Event.

1. Planning

2. Promoting

3. Running

4. Follow-up

5. Debrief

1. **Planning-** You'll want to start planning six to eight weeks prior to running your event. This gives you a longer runway, so you have time to create the assets you need to put in place. I like to see this as a reverse-engineering process. Start with the end in mind. Ultimately, where do you want people to go, and what do you want them to do at the end of the event? What is the offer? Is it to fill a group program or a call to explore working with you 1:1? Join a mastermind?

i. What is the start date for the program you are offering?

1. **The timeline for your Nurture Event**

Once you have the start date for the program you are selling, look at six to eight weeks before that start date if this is the first time you are running an online event. If you have done this before and already have assets created, you can just start using those assets to promote your event. Take two weeks to create the assets we went over earlier in the chapter.

2. **Promoting- This is the runway to your event.** Four weeks prior to your live virtual event, start promoting it in as many places as possible. Please give yourself enough promotional time. Three weeks is the minimum. Remember, it is a numbers game. Only a certain number of people who register will actually show up live. So the more people that you get in front of the better.

The numbers look like this. If 100 people register, only 30% typically show up. That means 30 people will show up live. Out of those 30, on average, only about 20%-30% will purchase your offer. That's about six to nine people who buy. Is that what you need? If not, adjust the numbers so you are clear on how many people need to register to convert to paying clients.

If you don't have enough people coming to your event, the actual event won't really matter. The big thing to keep in mind during this promotional period is to create as much visibility as you can. One great way to do this is with ONE-word marketing. This is a simple way to have your ideal client raise their hand in your ecosystem, then you share with some a high-value freebie and then follow up with them to invite them to join your free nurture event. Here's how it could look. For my ideal clients who are coaches and holistic practitioners who are starting their businesses, the number one question they have is, "Where do I find clients." So, I created a free guide called "Where to Find Clients in any Economy." Then, I created a Facebook post asking, "Who wants my free Where to find Clients in any Economy guide? Comment CLIENTS below, and I'll send your way." The ONE word I am asking them to share in the comments is CLIENTS. That's why it's called one-word marketing. When the person comments, it allows me to see who is raising their hand for my freebie. Then I message them and share the freebie. The beauty of this is that the more people comment, the more Facebook shows this to more people. It works with their algorithm. Each time someone comments, it pushes the post up to the front again. It can have a lasting value of weeks because of this. A few days after I send them the freebie, I follow up with them, and let them know we have a free event coming up that they may be interested in since they wanted the "Where to find Clients in any Economy" guide. I shared with them that I would be diving more deeply into how they can find clients in the free training and asked if I could share the link with them. Asking for permission is key. It allows them to feel in control and not feel like they are being spammed. And it shows that you really care about them.

You will also want to think about where else you can share this event online and who can help you share this with their communities. Collaboration partners are super helpful with this piece. Just remember, you want a partner who has your ideal audience but serves them in a different way than you do.

Example: If you are a health coach, you could collaborate with an energy worker, sound healer, yoga studio, or fitness professional. All of these would have an audience of people who are into self-improvement and wellness and would benefit XYZ.

Your main goal for this 3–4-week period is getting people registered for your event.

3. **Running-** This is the delivery of your event. It's where people will show up to your Zoom room, and you will stream this to your Facebook group for people who just want to watch but don't want to join on Zoom. (You can look online to get clear instructions on how to set this up.) Your Facebook group will also house the recording since you are streaming it there. You will be teaching your signature system and also inviting people to take the natural next step to work with you. Here is an example of what it might look like for you.

Day 1- Teach Step One

Day 2- Teach Step Two - Open enrollment to the offer at the end of the event.

Day 3- Recap the offer from the previous day and teach Steps Three and Four.

Day 4- Recap the offer from the previous day and teach any remaining steps

Day 5- This is a BONUS day. Have a Q&A Day and invite a previous client to share how you have helped them on their journey. Remind people of the offer and how it helps them have the solution they are looking for. If you have a special pricing bonus or early bird bonus, remind them of it.

Let's talk about bonuses for a minute. I like to have a bonus stack when running my live events. A bonus stack is extra freebies that you will offer to the attendees. People need reasons to say YES to themselves and bonuses help that process. They create extra value and also a sense of urgency as they are time-limited.

I always have both a pricing bonus that lasts 48 hours once enrollment is open and a value-related bonus. Some ideas for value-related bonuses are:

A fast-track strategy call with you, a bonus day of training, a special group experience, or access to a course or training, to name a few. The key is to keep it valuable and congruent with what they want. What would help them on their path to transformation quicker that they would absolutely LOVE?

You can also have an additional bonus come in the middle of your enrollment period. It's natural for people to buy at the beginning to get the early bird pricing and bonuses and at the end when the cart is about to close. So having something in the middle that is extra special, can help more people say yes. You will, of course, let the people who purchased earlier have access to this, too.

4.**Follow-Up-** OK, you have now run your event and opened enrollment to your offer. Now what? The fortune is in the follow-up. Download the list of everyone who registered for your event. This is your warm audience. These are the people who were the most interested in hearing how you could help them. So, it's time to follow up with all the ones who did not purchase your offer.

I like to keep it high touch and simple. Follow-up can be as simple as a message in Facebook Messenger or a private email to them asking them how they liked the event. What golden nuggets did they get from it? What did they find most valuable? What action steps were they inspired to take from the event?

Then, I ask them if they would like to "explore" joining me in the x,y,z program. If they say not at this time, I say thank you. And if they are open to it, I ask them to share with me what would have made it a yes for them. This allows me to have valuable feedback so I can be sure to speak about those reasons the next time I run the event.

If they say yes, I share my scheduling link with them and invite them into a 20-minute clarity call to see if this program or offer is the best fit for them and to answer any questions they may have. This is a no-pressure call with no obligation to buy. My only intention is to help them make an empowered decision. Either way, they will get value out of the call and feel clear about whatever they decide. We will talk more about this in the next chapter on making invitations. Remember, the energy you are coming from is SERVICE. Not to try to overpower or drag someone across the finish line.

5. **Debrief-** This final phase allows you to assess how the event went from a place of curiosity. We are not looking at "what went wrong." We want to ask ourselves three specific questions.

i. What went well that you are super excited to repeat?

ii. What went "Meh," and where do you see an opportunity to improve?

iii. What would you not want to repeat, and what are you willing to let go of?

This feedback is what allows you to hone and master your process. We are never experts the first time we run something. And we can't expect ourselves to fit into some idealist version of perfection. We want to see this as an opportunity for growth.

The key performance indicators (KPIs) we want to look at post-event are:

• Where did we promote the event?

• Where did people come from who joined the event?

• What was the conversion rate on the registration page? (the number of people who viewed it divided by the number of people who registered) We are looking for 30% or higher.

• Did it get in front of the right audience?

- How many people registered?

- How many showed up live?

- How many people purchased?

The answers to these will help us determine specifically how we want to improve the next time we run an event.

For example, was the conversion rate on the registration page low? Then, we can look at the copy and see if the wording is compelling and attractive to encourage our ideal client to register. Or maybe it's not the copy at all. Maybe we didn't share it where our ideal client was hanging out and didn't get enough people to actually see it? Did we personally invite people to the event or just expect them to know about it?

As empowered leaders, we get to pivot, tweak, hone, and master the process. When we look at it from this perspective, every event is a win because we are constantly learning.

Other types of common online Nurture Events

- Challenges- These are events that can take place for a certain number of days and focus on helping your ideal clients take action soon a daily basis to move them closer to the results they desire.

- Summits- These are typically online with a group of experts who are teaching their expertise. There is a host who runs it, and everyone shares the event to get a greater reach of people attending.

• Evergreen Webinars- These are recordings of training that people can access at any time. They register on a landing page and are then sent the recording of the free training.

Each one of these has its own process and formula for success. I recommend that you work with a business coach who has had success with the type of virtual event you want to run. I don't recommend doing these on your own as there are many moving pieces, and you need someone to guide you through the process. Summits and evergreen webinars are more advanced marketing strategies that require a team of support in order to run successfully.

So start with a talk either in person or online, and then go from there. The hardest part is deciding. And the biggest bottleneck is fear and self-doubt. The truth is you CAN do this. You DO have something valuable to bring to your audience and they do need to hear it from YOU.

Your next step is to decide. How will you nurture your audience so they have an experience of you? Will you choose an in-person talk or an online talk?

Regardless of what type of nurture event you decide to do, make sure to guide people back to your Facebook Group. People need an online platform to connect with you. I've had many clients tell me they have been following me on Facebook for years. It is only because of my online presence and community that I have been able to continue to connect and build the relationships with them that guided them from stranger to viewer to potential client to paying client.

In this chapter, you learned:

• The value of nurturing your audience.

• The different types of in -person and online nurturing events you can do.

• The importance of multiple contacts with a potential client.

• The importance of teaching your signature system in your event.

• How to keep an online presence where people can continue to connect with you.

In the next chapter, we will cover how to invite people to work with you and to make heart-centered sales. I'll take you through the ladder of beliefs that we all go through before we say yes to investing in anything and how to make these invitations in ways that feel amazing for you and your ideal clients. No slimy tactics or overcoming objections are required.

Chapter 8
Step 5-INVITE

"Dreams don't work unless you do." – **Maya Angelou.**

The final piece of the Nurture Method is INVITE.

Breaking the cycle of scarcity.

I remember a fundraiser I attended years ago to raise money to provide beds for kids who are forced to sleep on the floor because their families don't have the means to buy them a bed. Having a bed is such a common comfort for many; however, many impoverished families go without one.

The room was electric. Men were dressed in tuxedos. Women were dressed in fancy gowns or cocktail dresses. The room was decorated in elegant dining ware. And then the bidding started. The auctioneer came on and went through the list, with every person having a paddle to bid on the item of their choice. It was fun to watch the bids go higher and higher for the vacation home that was being bid upon. People were raising their paddles to inform the auctioneer that they wanted to bid, and there was a three-way bidding war happening. The price kept rising, the auctioneer going back and forth between all three until, finally there were only two people bidders left. It was exciting watching the dollar amount get higher and higher, way past the value of what the vacation home would have normally rented for. There were gasps with each increase and, finally, a winner. I even got caught up in the excitement and made a bid for several things myself. And yet, when I looked around, I saw something that troubled me.

The people making the big bids were men.

I'm not bashing men. I'm thankful for their generosity. It's just that where were the women?

Sure, there were some. I raised my paddle a few times to jump in the game.

But where were the women with the big money to donate?

We were missing out on 50% of the gender that can contribute to making our world better.

It was actually a bit of a shock- because, in the rooms I am in most often, the money makers are women. They are ambitious, high-achieving women committed to playing a bigger game to receive and give. Some are even the breadwinners for the family.

While I was sitting there, I had an epiphany. What if we could bring MORE women to the table of generosity?

In order to do that it requires women entrepreneurs to step up and step into their power. To claim their value and worthiness to receive for their gifts. Because when they receive abundance, they give abundantly. They are generous with their time and treasures. As a matter of fact, one of my colleagues just shared that she wants to make LOTS and LOTS of money so she can give 90% of it away and live comfortably on 10%.

This is why I'm doing the work I do.

To not only help women entrepreneurs create wealth and financial INDEPENDENCE but to urge them to take a seat at the table and make our world a better place for all. So they can do things like start the scholarships, give to the charities, and provide resources to the causes they most care about.

In order to do that, you must be willing to *make sales and profit in your business.* This chapter is designed to help you step up and step into your power and be the abundant feminine leader we need in this world.

Now, I am going to work through how you can break the cycle of scarcity, step into your purpose, and serve the people who are looking for you and need what you offer.

Making Soulful Invitations

You can't have a business if you don't invite people to work with you, and yet so many women get stuck here. I want to help you break out of the "starving healer" archetype and finally step into allowing yourself to be well-paid and feel amazing when you are inviting people to work with you.

Let's get clear on the purpose of making invitations. It's not about you. When you are inviting someone to have your support, you are helping them OFF of the "pain island" where they struggle and into a new possibility for their health and their life. It's in service to THEM and a sale becomes a side effect of the invitation of support. If you never invite them off of Pain Island to have your support to create a new transformation, you are abandoning them in their pain. And that is the opposite of heart-centered and service-driven. Let's start with the premise that making invitations is actually a service to others and that there IS a way to invite people to work with you and make sales in a way that aligns with your values and integrity.

Invite= Heart-Centered Sales

Now that you've attracted a potential client into your ecosystem, have nurtured them with value and built trust, it's time to make the invitation to work with you. Without this, no clients are having their lives transformed or finding a way out of their pain.

And in reality- if you don't have any clients, you don't have a business. What you have is an expensive hobby that serves no one. Invitations must be a part of your daily income-generating activities.

But before we dive in, let's make sure we are in alignment with the energy of making soulful sales. I hear from my clients that they want more paying clients, but they don't want to feel sales-y in the process of asking for the sale. The thing to remember here is that *sales-y is not an action.* It's an energy. So, if you don't want to feel sales-y, make sure you are not in the energy of being sales-y and that you ARE in the energy of serving.

174

Let's take another look at our formula:

Inner Game (Mindset) + Outer Game (Strategy) = Abundance.

INNER GAME

The energy of who we are when we invite someone to work with us is our inner game. The mindset we are in and the beliefs we are thinking create our feeling state.

What do you want to FEEL when inviting someone to work with you? I like to feel confident, generous, in service, helpful, caring, etc.

In order to feel those things about making invitations, you must have a **belief plan.**

Your belief plan is a series of three to five beliefs that you choose to think about yourself, the value you provide, the clients you serve, and the impact you are here to make. For example, when you have the belief that your clients get results faster if they work with you, than they can on their own, that allows you to make invitations gracefully and easily.

Very often, the reason my clients don't like having sales conversations is because they make it about them and not the client. They are worried about what someone will think about them. They feel awkward asking for money and make it about the money instead of the actual transformation that gets to happen with their client. But what if you could see that inviting someone to work with you is actually in service to help them create the transformation they desire? It has nothing at all to do with you. You are merely the vehicle to helping them say yes to themselves and yes to the result they desire.

Approaching conversations with clients like this flips the conversation on its head and makes it your moral and ethical responsibility to invite someone to work with you. Especially if you have a way to help someone out of their pain.

What you are doing when inviting someone out of their pain is helping them make an empowered decision about what *they* are going to do to get to the other side. You cannot decide for them. You can't decide if they can afford it or not. You simply have to help them see the various options that are available to them and will support their goals. What level of support are they looking for? What is their timeline for wanting the results? Do they want a group program, course, or a private coach package? Ultimately, the decision is theirs to make. The good news is that there is no manipulation or pushing required. You don't need to overcome anyone's objections or overpower them to get them to buy. Helping them make a yes or no decision is the best thing you can do for someone who is struggling. If they are a yes, then you help them decide what offer of yours is the best fit for them. If they are a no, you can guide them to the support or resources outside of your business that can help them get what they want. But leaving them sitting on the fence creates no movement at all for them. All it does is allow them to continue to sit in their pain.

Let me share with you my three-step process to align with the energy that I desire to be in when inviting someone to enroll with me.

• **Step 1- Create a belief plan with high emotion. What is the FEELING I desire to feel when I am having a conversation about how I can help someone get the results they desire by working with me? Personally, I like to feel calm, confident and supportive.**

o Here is a sample of some of the beliefs I use to feel calm, confident, and supportive.

o Making a sale is a side effect of being of service and helping someone else get what they want.

o I am authentic and full of integrity when having a conversation and making an invitation.

o I have an opportunity to enrich someone's life with my work.

o People WANT to be invited.

o It's my moral responsibility to invite them into a new way to get out of their pain.

o There are so many people who need my help right now.

o People are looking for the exact solution I provide and are waiting for me to invite them.

o Making invitations is easy. I get to be a stand for my potential client.

o Premium prices are reassuring for my clients.

o Premium prices create greater commitment and better results.

o Premium prices mean I can work with fewer clients and create amazing outcomes.

o My clients love me.

o Everything is Totally working out for me!

o I have the support of the entire Universe!

o The Universe Totally has my back!

o I am Totally & Always taken care of!

o I am a powerful & resourceful creator!

o I am one with infinite genius, omnipresent ideas & possibilities of Success!

Pick a few that most resonate with you and say them out loud. How do they feel? What emotions do you feel in your body?

Our beliefs create our perception of our world, ourselves, and others. When we change our beliefs, we create a state change and create a new identity of who we are in the world. We shift from believing one thing about ourselves that prevents the outcome we desire into believing the thought about ourselves or the circumstance that helps us get closer to our desired goal.

For example, before you can create a $10,000 month, you have to have the belief that you are capable of creating that. Even if you haven't done it yet. There needs to be the belief that it's possible for you. If you hold the belief that it's not possible, no strategy in the world will work. So often, people think they first have to have their $10,000 per month in order to see that it's possible. Remember the saying, "Seeing is believing?" That's not how we actually create in this world. There must first be the thought of the *possibility* of what you desire. Then, the action taken towards that possibility and finally the result of the action. We create this way all day on autopilot without even thinking about it.

Remember the man who ran the first four-minute mile? Before he broke that record, no one believed it was possible. So, no one ran the mile quicker. But he did believe in the possibility of running a four-minute mile. He believed he could, and then he took action toward it by training, and finally, he accomplished his goal. He believed he could, and he did. And when he broke that record, runner after runner also ran the four-minute mile. Because of him and the fact that he achieved that goal, they were able to believe it was possible, too. That's the power of our beliefs. They not only change our lives, but they change the lives of others too. You have to initiate those beliefs to support what you desire first. You can't just wait for success to come to you. Otherwise, you're creating more by your reaction to

Christine Williams

circumstances and less on purpose. Remember the thought model I shared earlier? Our thoughts create feelings. And our feelings create action, inaction, or reactions. And those lead to a result. So, what we see in front of us today is based on that thought model. Most often, we unconsciously react to a circumstance. Something happens, and we have a thought about what that means. Then, we have a feeling and react to that feeling. But when we can be intentional about our thoughts and choose how we want to feel so that we take the action that supports our goals, the outcome changes. Anything is possible if you just believe it is.

- **Step 2- Visualize the outcome, not the how.**

This is actually really fun. I call it future pulling. Create a movie in your mind of the outcome that you desire actually happening. Notice where you are, who you are with, what you are feeling, seeing, and experiencing. Turn up the dial on your senses. I like to imagine that I'm stepping into the body of the future person who already has what I want. I see myself smiling and having a relaxed conversation. I see the person I'm speaking with excited to step into her transformation. She is saying," Yes, I can't wait to get started. How can I pay? When can I have my first call with you?" The invitation is easy and flowing, and I get to be fully present to see my potential client excited about the new possibilities that are waiting for her with my help. Seeing this in my mind before it happens creates a feeling of calm, confidence, and the excitement of serving a new client. And, those feelings also help my client feel safe when I am talking to her.

Our clients pick up on our feelings. When we are worried, lack confidence, or are in the energy of needing to GET a client, they feel that. And that feels unsafe to them. It's why you get that hint sometimes that something just feels off when you have an interaction with someone. You are picking up on their energy. But when someone is relaxed and confident, you feel that too and want to be around them. You feel safe. You resonate with their energy. That's the way we want our clients to feel when we are having a conversation with them and why the inner work is so important for us to do prior to any sales call.

OUTER GAME- The Ladder Of Beliefs

On the practical side of the strategy of inviting people to work with you, there is a ladder of beliefs that everyone climbs before they can be a YES. When we understand this belief ladder, we can see how to support someone in making an empowered decision and not about "closing the deal.' As I mentioned in the inner game, invitations are about how you can help your potential client create their transformation. So the heart-centered strategy that results in soulful exchanges is to find out where they might be stuck on the ladder of beliefs and how that is keeping them from being a yes to themselves. Then, we figure out how to help them move through it.

When my clients first learn this ladder of beliefs, they feel such a sense of relief. They realize that they don't have to sell themselves or try to convince someone they need their service. Instead, it gets to be a supportive conversation that the potential client will walk away from feeling completely heard, valued, and supported in their decision.

Let's dive into the ladder of beliefs that everyone climbs before making any buying decision.

The base of your ladder must begin with YOU being enrolled in yourself. In order to guide someone to make an empowered decision, you must believe in yourself and the value you are bringing. It's your energy and confidence that will guide the process, so be sure to go back to your belief plan before supporting someone in an enrollment conversation.

Here are the rungs on the Ladder of Beliefs. I learned this from my first business coach, Kaela Gedda.

1.I believe it's possible in the world

2.I believe it's possible for me

3.I believe it's possible for me now- not later.

4.I believe it's possible for me now, and I desire your support

5.I believe it's possible for me now, with your support, and I am willing to explore resources or other support to make the investment possible.

Let's break down these steps on the ladder a bit more.

- **Step 1- I believe it's possible in the world.**

o In order for anyone to be a YES to working with you, they need to believe that the results they desire are possible in the world we live in. If they don't believe that what they desire is possible, they will never continue to climb the ladder. It will always be a "no" for them. For example, If you have a potential client who wants to feel energized and finally love the skin she is in, she needs to believe that other people have accomplished that, too. She needs to see if it's possible in the world somewhere. Sharing client success stories goes a long way in helping potential clients see that the result they want is actually happening for others, too.

- **Step 2- I believe it's possible for me.**

o The next step on the ladder is the belief that it's also possible for them. They can visualize and see themselves actually having the result they desire. If they can't see it for themselves, they can't move on. So, helping them visualize what will change for them when they achieve their goal is critical. Asking them questions about what their future will look like when they have their transformation will allow them to step into their own belief of what this future can look like, not only for them but also for those they love. You're helping to paint a picture of not just what it looks like but what it might also feel like and the emotions they have when they finally step off pain island and onto pleasure island. I'll share a list of questions that I use with potential clients at the end of this chapter to help you with this process.

- **Step 3- I believe it's possible for me now.**

o The next step is to help them see that NOW is the time for them to make the transformation. Not when all the stars align, the kids finally go away to college, or everyone else thinks it's the right thing for them to do so. They need to see that NOW is their time and that there is a cost in waiting. Not only for themselves but for those around them. What happens if your potential client waits to lower their cholesterol or waits to make any lifestyle changes that will help them feel more energized? There is always a personal cost to putting things off. So, ask your potential clients why NOW is the perfect time for them to make this change. And what might be the consequences of waiting. Once they answer these questions, they will see why NOW is the time.

• Step 4- I believe it's possible for me now, and I desire your support.

o Now that your potential clients can see and believe it's possible for them, the next step is for them to feel like YOU are the one to help them. She can't say YES to having your support until she feels a sense of trust and belief that you can help. This belief is built by feeling safe, heard, valued, and guided in the conversation. Remember, people won't say yes unless they trust you. Repeating back clearly in their own words what they have said in the conversation helps them feel heard and valued. Sharing client success stories or case studies helps them see that you have a track record of helping people with their problems and that people get results with you and your process.

- **Step 5- I'm ready and willing to explore resources or support in my decision to invest.**

o This is the last step before a YES can take place. Sometimes, this shows up as a money issue. But in reality, it's a trust issue. Maybe they don't believe they will follow through. Maybe they don't feel worthy of using money for themselves or their health. It's so much easier to just say, "I can't afford it," than to confront the real issue, which is I can't spend money on myself. Or - What if I fail again? The truth is, there IS money for what we value most. I've seen it over and over again with my clients. Once they are a YES to their transformation, and feel worthy to have it, they are willing to explore resources to support themselves in having it. Sometimes, that might look like having a conversation with a partner or spouse. Sometimes, it looks like getting resourceful to see where money may be that they hadn't thought of. The important thing here is to help them see that there are so many possibilities for them to have this support because they are worthy of having their desires. That includes being worthy of the resources to invest in their transformation.

If a client is a heart YES for having the transformation and wants to work with you but needs help figuring out the financial investment, you can ask them if they are open to having support to come up with potential resources. A fun way to open to potential resources and options that I have used over and over again when I wanted to invest, but my bank account said no is called "50 ways." I learned it from my friend and coach, Sara Connell. It works because it takes the focus off LACK and into possibilities. It works with your Reticular Activating System, the part of your brain that seeks evidence and experiences for what you're looking for. It tells our brain that there actually IS a way to achieve this goal and opens us to abundant possibilities.

Here's how to play. On a piece of paper, at the top, write the dollar goal needed. Then write all the ways that amount could be generated. Any idea counts. It's a brainstorming session. You're not committing to do any of them yet, you're just tapping into creative resourcing and co-creation. What ends up happening is that out of all the potential ways to make money to support the goal, a few will actually sound like things to try. And THIS is huge for your clients. It takes them out of being a victim of their circumstances and believing they are stuck in their circumstance into an empowered state to create what they need.

I will forever be grateful to my first business coach, who helped me through this. I knew I wanted her support, I believed I was worthy to have the support, but my bank account said no. I literally only had $100 to put down to say YES to a $10,000 investment in her group program. She asked me if I was a heart yes and did I wanted support to come up with ways I could find the investment. I said YES. So, I brainstormed several possibilities and came up with one I wanted to take action on. I knew I needed $900 for the first payment, so I wrote down how I could come up with $900 and decided to invite people to work with me in a 6-week group wellness program. I made a list of 25 people I thought might be interested and personally reached out to them. Five of them said YES. And within a week, I had created $1,000. I was never again beholden to my bank account because I learned that I could create whatever I needed whenever I needed it. That one lesson has served me so well over the years. And I truly believe it is why I am here today to share this book with you. If I had just said 'I don't have the money, I can't afford it," I would not have the coaching business I have today. Because of that decision, I get to help women step out of limiting circumstances and into abundant possibilities, just like I did. My coach was a stand for my possibilities, not my fear or doubt. Being a stand for your client's dreams and vision is one of the most loving things you can offer them. I believe we are all capable of creating the resources we need. There is always a way. It all depends on if we really want it and if we are willing to do the work to find it.

Lastly, I want to speak about the idea of choosing the clients that you feel most excited to support, because it directly relates to your identity of being an abundant and empowered leader. Decide now that you will only accept clients and invite clients to work with you if you can help create the transformations they desire the most. When you come from this mindset, you will be out of the lack, fear and scarcity. You grow in abundance when you stop just taking on any client who wants to work with you and focus instead on working with the people who you truly want to support. You don't need to accept anyone into your practice. You're not trying to get a client at all costs. Your life and your business will succeed so much better when you are in alignment with inviting people to work with you who are the best fit to get the results with the service you provide. And that takes the neediness out of any mutual fit call. How would your business change if it was LESS about closing the deal and more about seeing if you could serve someone most effectively and help them make an empowered decision? For me and my clients, it created a feeling of relaxed confidence, calm, peace, and opportunities that make a six-figure business not only possible but a joy to wake up to every day.

The "HOW TO's" of inviting.

Inviting people to work with you can be so easy and yet so many overcomplicate this. I've created five-figure sales days simply by reaching out in person to invite my warm audience into an opportunity that I feel would truly benefit them. Because they have already intentionally come into my ecosystem, and been nurtured, this is simply inviting them to explore possibilities that are available to help them get the result they are looking for. Sometimes, I do this directly via Facebook Messenger, sometimes I reach out directly by email, and sometimes with a voice message. The important thing here isn't the method of delivery. It's the actual invitation.

Before you make any invitations, first decide on the offer you want to invite people to explore. We start here because we are clear on the people who would most benefit, and in order to do that, we need to know what the offer is.

Then, make your list of 50-100 people who are in your warm or hot audience. These are people in your Facebook group, those who have come to a workshop or event, those who have downloaded a freebie, those who have connected with you in some way expressing interest on social media, or even current or past clients. We are not doing cold reachouts here. We are not inviting people into a free coaching session. We are not spamming 100 people in the DM's who have no idea who we are.

We are intentionally reaching out to the people who would most benefit from the offer, who like and trust us, and inviting them to explore it because this specific offer would help them get the result they are most looking for. Notice I'm talking about THEM and the result they want. I'm not leading with a reach out of "Would you like to join my 12-week program for $3,000." That's about YOU, not them. Instead make it based on a result or a transformation that they would like to have. For example: "Hey Chris, I'm so glad to have you with us inside my free Facebook group. I noticed you joined me in the workshop *"How to Find Paying Clients in Any Economy."* Would you like to explore ways to consistently bring paying clients into your programs or offers? I have a new resource that I think would be just the right fit for you if you're looking for more support to implement what I taught in the workshop. Just let me know, and we can hop on a quick chat to see if this is the best fit for you to reach your goals." This type of reach-out feels so much better than trying to convince someone to buy your offer and listing all the features that it comes with. When you reach out to only your warm audience and from the energy of service and matching resources to their needs, the invitations become fun, and easy and soulful exchanges naturally happen.

Invitations can also happen during your virtual workshop or live event. As a matter of fact, I highly recommend that you send your offer if you are doing a virtual workshop or live event.

Christine Williams

Seeding your offer simply means letting them know at the beginning of your talk or workshop that you will share a valuable resource later that will help them implement what they are learning if they would like more support. This prepares them in advance for your heart-centered offer and feels less like a pitch. They are actually wondering what the resource may be, and you are now in a position to just share what it is, at the time you open enrollment. It's easy. Think of it like offering them a cookie or a dessert at a party. The value is in making the offer, not the end result. They can certainly say no. We don't get bent out of shape or judge ourselves as unworthy if someone doesn't want the dessert. We just move on to the next person at our party. It's the same for your offers. People want to be invited. So simply make the invitation without making the answer mean something about you or your value. Your value and worth are non-negotiable. If someone isn't ready for it now, they may be at a later time. I always tell my clients, no just means not now. And it's always about them and their belief along the belief ladder, not about the value of the service.

When my client Stephanie started doing this in her business, she enrolled more clients into her group program and made more income in the first four months of 2024 than she did in all of 2023. She went from being afraid to invite someone to work with her to feel confident and in service to the people who had come into her world to learn from her. She made more invitations to connect, had more conversations about how she could help them, and invited them to hear the details of the options that would be the best fit for them. It became easy, and she no longer dreaded inviting someone into a conversation or exploring working with her.

In this chapter, you learned:

• Making soulful exchanges with potential clients requires you to be willing to step out of the cycle of scarcity and step into your identity as an abundant leader.

• People don't have objections. They have false beliefs about their worthiness to receive, their ability to follow through, or their power to create the resources they need. The importance of being a stand for your potential client and not for the fearful circumstance or story they are in.

• People want to be invited.

• To make the offer about THEM and the transformation they want, not the features or the price of your program.

• To specifically select your clients from your warm audience to invite into conversations.

• Seeding your offers often leads to more clients saying yes to working with you.

• Someone's NO is not a no to you. It's a no to themselves at this moment in time. They may be a YES later.

• Your self-worth and value are non-negotiable. Disentangle the invitation from the outcome.

In the next chapter, we will talk about empowered leadership and mastering the process to build and grow the business of your dreams.

Chapter 9
Step Six: EMPOWER

"You don't have to play masculine to be a strong woman." —
Mary Elizabeth Winstead.

"Above all, be the heroine of your life, not the victim." — **Nora
Ephron**

Here we are in the final step of the Soulful Abundance
System®. EMPOWER. This step is all about mastery and
sticking with the process of building your business. Being the
leader who is able to hone, tweak, pivot, and build the resilience
that creates success.

One thing I want to make super clear, I really don't believe
in failure. Maybe you've been doing this building business thing,
and it hasn't quite worked out like you thought. You might be
considering calling it quits or wondering if you have what it takes
to really build a Six-Figure business. I get it. I've been there.

There are times on this business journey that have been so
intoxicating I've had to pinch myself to see if it's real. At other
times, it has brought me to my knees, and I've wanted to burn it
all down and just grow veggies in the country, get off the grid,
and spend my time knitting and rocking on the front porch.

So, if you're thinking of throwing in the towel, let me say this: If you can't get the dream of having your own business out of your mind if making your own schedule and having the freedom to do as you wish without someone else telling you what time to arrive, how much you can make or what you "should" be doing is still on your heart; if the thought of being well paid by helping others lead happier healthier lives makes your eyes light up, then stick with it.

I invite you to let go of the FEAR of failure and actually see it as feedback that propels you forward toward your success. Be 100% responsible for your results without guilt or blame. Own anything that looks like a mistake, and CELEBRATE it because it means you've gotten off the starting line. You're doing hard things. You've upgraded from being on the bench as a spectator to being an official entrepreneur. And you're making it happen. In fact, if things were going smoothly ALL the time, I would say there is something bigger waiting for you.

That's the key to success. The gold comes from the things we learn from the times when things didn't work out like we thought they would. So we will try again. We pivot and try something else. We do it again and see what feedback we get from the results. We double down on what's working, let go of what doesn't light us up, and upgrade what feels like 'MEH.' But we don't quit. That's truly the only way you can fail. And if you quit in the midst of what you perceive as failure, you'll miss out on the greatest reward of all.

Don't be one of the many whose fear of failure has paralyzed them. Make the workbook even if there are spelling mistakes. Run the masterclass or workshop even if just one person shows up. Start the Facebook group even if you don't know what to post, what to say or have impostor syndrome whispering in your ears. Price your program and invite people into conversations. I promise you if you just take the shot, you are on your way to success. But if you never take the shot, that's guaranteed failure.

For this last chapter, let's take a look at eight obstacles of success and how you can BE the empowered leader and see these blocks for what they really are, an illusion and resistance to fulfilling your dreams.

Eight Obstacles to Success:

According to Steven Pressfield, "Resistance is a negative force in the world that keeps you from fulfilling your dreams. It's that voice in the back of your head that tells you that you aren't good enough, that you don't have enough time, or that it will never work.

Here are eight ways that resistance shows up to keep you from achieving Six-Figure success.

#1 Procrastination:

I think we all know this one quite well and have experienced it at one time or another. I tell my client that perfectionism is the birther to procrastination. We have this idea that something must be done perfectly before we can take action on it. So we wait and edit, and tweak, and try to get it just right. The problem is there is no perfect. There will always be an opportunity to improve or the next level to get to. What is the true meaning of procrastination?

Procrastination is the act of delaying or putting off tasks until the last minute or past their deadline. Some researchers define procrastination as a "form of self-regulation failure characterized by the irrational delay of tasks despite potentially negative consequences."

The way out of procrastination is actually through it. Procrastination is just an old habit of avoidance, so we don't feel a negative feeling. Overcoming it requires action. We tend to WAIT until we feel confident. But confidence is built upon actions. No one is confident when doing something for the first time. It's the repetition of the action over time that creates confidence. So when our brain is telling us to just wait until we feel confident, it's actually just wanting us to stay where we are, in our comfort zone. Unfortunately, nothing changes in your comfort zone. You have to step out of it in order to create change.

Notice what you are procrastinating on and break it down to the smallest step possible. When you take even the smallest action, you start to build momentum, and even the smallest motion creates more motion. There is a saying I learned early in my coaching career, "Small Hinges Swing Big Doors." Your actions don't need to be big giant leaps. They can be small steps that create just a 1% change forward. And if you think a 1% change can't make a difference, I want you to think about the airplane that flies off course. Just one degree off course from JFK in New York to LAX in California, you would wind up 40 miles off in the Pacific Ocean. Those small steps forward matter and without them, you'll stay right where you are.

Want to do that Facebook live but keep procrastinating? Let's break it down into small steps.

1. Pick a day and time and schedule it on your calendar.

2. Pick a topic that you feel you can talk about

3. Tell someone you're going to do it for accountability.

4. Go live for just two minutes on the topic of choice

5. Come back to your accountability partner and celebrate when it's done.

The more we procrastinate, the harder it gets to take action. The best thing we can do is commit to taking just one small step and be consistent in those small steps until the task is done.

#2 Over Analyzing or Rationalizing:

Rationalization is a defense mechanism. It is often a way to avoid making mistakes or placing ourselves in a negative light to avoid criticism from others. While rationality may help us solve problems and make decisions, it's important to balance it with creativity and imagination. Over-analysis can cause us to lose sight of the bigger picture and miss out on opportunities. It prevents any decision from being made and leads to decision fatigue, where no option seems right.

The way out is to stop focusing on past mistakes and what could go wrong and instead start focusing on the possibilities and positive outcomes. Placing your thoughts on the positive solution will unhook you from the fear of there needing to be a perfect decision. There's good ole' perfection again. And once you make your decision, LOVE it. Reinforce your decision with all the reasons why it's the BEST decision for you now. What you look for, you will find. So look for the reasons for your choices and remind yourself of them when fear rears its ugly head.

#3 Fear - Good Ole' fear:

Fear pops up ANYTIME we want to move in a new direction. It's actually an inner program that is wired into us from our ancestors. Our brain doesn't care about our happiness. It cares about our survival. And anything NEW threatens our sense of safety, love, and belonging - hence our survival. Think about it, if we were not on the lookout for dangers that might take us out - like the lion behind the bush - we would not live to see tomorrow. Same with our sense of belonging. Being a part of a tribe meant survival and access to resources like food, protection, and shelter. We needed the safety and love of our tribe. It was common for people to die if they were excommunicated from their tribe.

So, the way out is to see false fear as a thought error. True fear, like running away from a bear, is what we want to keep. But the fear of being visible so our business can grow is a false fear. We are not in danger of dying. Yet our brain gives us a thought error, which leads to a feeling of fear.

The way out is to acknowledge the fear for what it truly is. A thought error. There is nothing wrong with you. You've just had a thought from your brain that wants to keep you safe. Once you identify the fear as a thought error, you can create a NEW thought that feels better and helps you take the action anyway.

#4 Perfectionism - The good girl:

Perfectionists tend to be "all-or-nothing" thinkers. They see events and experiences as either good or bad, perfect or imperfect, with nothing in between. I call this "Black or White thinking." Such thinking often leads to procrastination because demanding perfection of oneself can quickly become overwhelming. Perfectionistic behaviors can increase one's vulnerability to depression, social anxiety, and other barriers to success. These blocks to productivity and success result from the perfectionist's focus on the final outcome. Instead of concentrating on the process of accomplishing a task, perfectionists focus exclusively on the outcome of their efforts. This relentless pursuit of the ultimate goal can seriously hinder their efforts. It creates future problems where none exist and stops any forward momentum of inspired action that leads to the results they desire.

The way out is to focus on the inspired action and not the end result. For example, instead of focusing on getting a YES to your offer, shift that and focus on the action of making the invitation. How many no's can you get? How many invitations can you make? Release the idea that there is one right way to do anything and get the win from taking the inspired action toward the result. Not getting the result itself. It takes practice to detach yourself from the outcome. To take action even if things are uncertain in how they will turn out. The beautiful thing is that on the other side of the action, you get feedback. So you can course correct and take the next step with new information.

#5 Giving Up:

There is a saying that "you are only three feet from gold." The meaning of this goes back to the gold miners. They would dig and dig and dig for days or weeks and just when they were about to strike it rich, they would give up. They couldn't see that they were so close. Giving up is the only way you can fail. Often we think it's easier to just give up and go get a 9-5 job rather than stay in the game and build your business. But in reality - you are never closer to success than you are right now. Thomas Edison tried 10,000 times to get the light bulb to work. It was on the 10,001st try that it worked. Can you imagine what our world would look like today without electricity to power our homes? So stay in the game. Find mentorship and a community that supports you when you want to sneak out the back door. I promise if you stick with it, greater things than you can imagine are possible for you.

#6 Imposter syndrome - hiding and playing small:

According to the National Institute of Health, "Imposter syndrome (IS) is a behavioral health phenomenon described as "self-doubt of intellect, skills, or accomplishments among high-achieving individuals. These individuals cannot internalize their success and subsequently experience feelings of self-doubt, anxiety, depression, and/or apprehension of being exposed as a fraud in their work, despite verifiable and objective evidence of their successfulness." If you have ever experienced imposter syndrome, welcome to the club. It will surely take you out if you let it. It actually leads to over-preparation and procrastination, so I see imposter syndrome as a cousin to perfectionism and fear.

The way out is to acknowledge the feelings and get clear on what the thoughts are that are making you feel like an imposter or fraud. Those thoughts are just another thought error. Often I see my clients struggling with this when they feel they have more work to do on themselves and are not where they want to be in their own health or wellness. One of my clients sabotaged herself over and over again because she felt like she still needed to lose 15 pounds. So, how could she help anyone else lose weight? The truth is that you don't need to have everything figured out or perfect before you can help someone else. As a matter of fact, no one has it perfect. You just need to make sure that you are a few steps ahead of who you are meant to help. I refer to this as being a few cars ahead on the freeway. We all have something to contribute and can help, no matter how much of a mess our brain *thinks* we are. The other step I invite you to take is to ask yourself, "Is that really true?" Is it

Christine Williams

really true that you need to lose weight before you can help someone else? If it can't be answered as a YES in a court of law, it's a thought error. NOT A FACT. A great exercise that you can do to identify imposter syndrome is to write down everything you are thinking on a piece of paper. What are all the reasons why you think you can't? What are the reasons why something didn't work out for you? What reason do you have that leads you to believe that you need to get yet another certification before you can start growing your business? Answer these questions truthfully, then go back and underline JUST THE FACTS. What you'll notice is that most of what you write is just a thought. And thoughts can be changed. Now, take the negative thoughts and for each one, write a positive version of it. By the end of the exercise you'll be feeling so much better because you will be thinking thoughts that help you feel powerful and capable.

I like to think of these two types of thoughts as two different trains. One train is going to the land of fear and one train is going to the land of possibility. When we slip into imposter syndrome, we just have to get off the "train of thought" that is taking us AWAY from where we want to go. Reframing your thoughts gets you onto the train of possibility and headed in the direction of a successful business.

#7 Self-Doubt and Unworthiness:

"There's something wrong with me. I'm too different." "It won't work for me." I call this the "Unicorn Syndrome." It's the thought error that tells us, "I'm too different for it to work for me." It shows up in some very sneaky ways when we see others

202

having success, and we are not. I hear my clients say things like," I'm just an energy worker, I'm not a coach, so I can't have a Six-Figure Business Model." Or, "I'm a coach, but I serve people who would never invest with me at a premium rate. People can't afford to work with me." It feels true, but in reality, it's all just another thought error and shows up as fighting for your perceived limitations instead of for what's really true. You are here to do the work that has been placed on your heart for a reason. You are needed, and the way you serve others is desperately needed in today's world.

The way out is through doing daily mindset work. Choosing NEW thoughts that create new beliefs, that allow you to feel confident. Your worthiness is non-negotiable. Nothing you do or don't do can take that away. If you were born, you are worthy. It's a birthright.

Take a moment to go back to the daily alignment practice in chapter 1 and create a better feeling set of thoughts that help you to feel calm, confident, and at peace and put those on repeat.

#8 Lone Wolf Syndrome-

"I just need to figure it out on my own." What's wrong with going it alone? Do you find yourself *stuck in the trap of trying to figure out every single step on your own*? Maybe you wait to take action until you've got all the pieces to the puzzle.

Here's the thing, there are two reasons to break out of being a lone wolf.

1. **You don't have to try to figure it out on your own.** In fact, you shouldn't. Instead, you can borrow someone else's 'how' and start seeing the results you desire now. The truth is that mastery requires 10,000 hours of practice or a decade of dedication. However, if you're like me, you likely don't have that kind of time (or patience). *I know I didn't as a single mom trying to get my business off the ground and pay the bills.*

But what if you could tap into someone else's expertise, someone who's already achieved what you want and is willing to share that with you?

Wouldn't that be amazing? No more throwing spaghetti at the wall to see what sticks.

You'd have a ***proven process*** that actually has been tried and proven to work.

Being supported by a mentor, coach, or program is always your shortcut to success. Because **success leaves clues.**

And I'm not talking about being a cookie-cutter copycat. I'm talking about using a proven system; **you can make your own** with expert guidance on exactly how to do that.

Others have already put in the hard work, taken the risks, made the mistakes, and fine-tuned the process so you don't have to. Investing to benefit from their wisdom and getting results now, not later, will provide a very good return on your investment, more so than any other investment you could make for your business.

You invest once, you keep the knowledge for YEARS (and compound the results).

As a matter of fact, I still return to principles I learned years ago from past coaching programs. Investing in mentorship has a lifetime value. Not just value during the time you are in the course or program.

2. Having support collapses the learning curve.

Our culture often glorifies the idea of figuring everything out independently, which can often slow you down on your road to getting the results you want. I call this the "LONE WOLF SYNDROME."

Instead of waiting years while you TRY to figure it out on your own, you can achieve your goals in days or months by borrowing someone else's proven method. You create clarity quicker and take action sooner, which leads directly to your results.

If this resonates with you, I'd like for you to take a moment to reflect on the areas in your business where you're STUCK and trying to navigate the 'how' on your own and ask yourself: "Is this the best use of my precious time? If I could have done it on my own, wouldn't I have done that already?" Then, ask yourself: "How fast could my business grow if I invested in myself by borrowing someone else's success system?"

This, my friend, is the recipe for exponential growth and success, and not in some distant future, but right now. Even at the stage of my business now where I'm incredibly successful, I still invest in coaching and mentorship. I have a book coach, a mindset coach, and a business coach. Plus, I'm in other communities with my peers so that I can be surrounded by positive examples of building and growing my business. Going it alone is taking the long road to success. And let me tell you, it's not cheaper to do it yourself. How many times has it taken you days, weeks, or months to figure something out when a coach or mentor could have helped you with it in moments. They are sharing not only their knowledge, but they know the challenges ahead of you and can help you navigate them BEFORE it turns into a problem. This not only saves you time, but just think about the loss of sales, loss of confidence, and loss of money you could experience by having to go back and fix the mistake that could have been avoided.

I've been so blessed to be able to share my system with 1000s of women in my coaching programs and with you in this book. If you'd like more support to help you implement this system in a way that is customized for you, just click this link, and we will set up a time for you to chat with a member of my team to guide you to the resources that will be the BEST help to you. https://ShinewithChris.as.me/clarity

Three strategies to avoid going it alone:

1. Who has accomplished what you want to do (in a way that inspires you)? Look for three people who are seven times ahead of you in their business.

2. Who mentors or coaches on the specific thing that you want to achieve and has a simple system or process you can follow?

3. What communities are living the vision and life you want to live?

Write the answers to these questions down and use the answers to take your next action step.

Our final step in my Soulful Abundance System® circles back around to where we started. Aligning to the IDENTITY and beliefs of what we desire as this next stage of business.

To help you, here are **12 Abundant and Empowered Leader Paradigms** that will remind you of your identity as an abundant and empowered leader. I invite you to print these out and place them somewhere where you can see them as a reminder of WHO you are being. (Download them here in the resource portal.)

This is the QR code for the resource portal.

When we align to these paradigms we are actually using Neuroscience to help us create our success. Here's how neuroscience plays a factor in helping you to take action and create the results that you WANT and not what you don't want.

Neuroscience is the study of the brain and nervous system and their functions in creating your beliefs, making decisions, and taking action. It's what happens in the brain when we have emotions, or thoughts, or when we create art or music, or when we read and write, and these things impact our behavior. If you remember back to the THOUGHT MODEL in chapter one, our thoughts about something create feelings, and our feelings create actions, inaction, or reactions, which lead to results. So, anything we are seeing now in our life or business is a result of the thoughts we put on repeat the most, how they make us feel, and the actions we took or didn't take towards our goals. It's why mindset work is so important to your success and is a critical component of the Soulful Abundance System® in creating the success you desire.

Neuroscience research shows that the brain is incredibly adaptable and capable of rewiring itself in response to our experiences, behaviors, and environmental influences. This is known as neuroplasticity, and it is at the foundation of our ability to learn, unlearn & relearn throughout our lives. It literally reorganizes itself continually as we experience life. So, if we want to create success, we need to rewire any false beliefs of limitations that may be getting in our way and install NEW beliefs that inspire us to take action on the things that create the results we desire. The interesting thing here is that it's not just about the words but also the FEELINGS you have when you are thinking about them. The brain loves to save energy. This means that it looks for ways to align our thoughts so that they are recurrent and on automatic pilot the majority of the time. A thought takes energy, so in order to save energy, the most dominant thoughts you think are put into the subconscious and become the basics of our belief system. Our belief system is how we think about and see the world, ourselves, and others. Cultivating a growth mindset views setbacks as a stepping stone to success rather than a reflection of your abilities, value, or worthiness. Paradigms, affirmations and choosing the beliefs that feel good help us to do this.

Even if you don't yet believe them, there is power in repetition and creating new neural pathways until you DO believe the positive thoughts. So go ahead and read them aloud every day. Repetition builds belief. It's one of the reasons why we see the same commercial on Superbowl Sunday a gazillion times. You know what I mean, like that pizza commercial that plays over and over again, and then all of a sudden, you want pizza for dinner. That's the power of repetition. And we are already repeating messages about ourselves in our heads all day, every day. The problem is most of us are not being intentional when we are doing it. What you focus on grows. Your brain will look for evidence to support your beliefs and thoughts. Have you ever noticed a certain color car? And all of a sudden, you start seeing this color everywhere? That's our brain looking for evidence to support our belief. It happened to me recently when I was looking for a new car. I was researching a certain brand of car and began seeing them everywhere. On the freeway, in my neighborhood, in parking lots. My brain was filtering what was coming into my awareness. There were not really more of these cars all around. It was just my attention. My Reticular Activating System was working to bring me more of what I was thinking about. That's pretty cool unless we have beliefs about ourselves, others, or the world that bring evidence to our awareness that we are not good enough, are a failure, can't do it, won't be liked, or are self-critical. This is old subconscious programming that plays in the background. We don't even notice it.

If we want to BE abundant, successful, and empowered leaders, we have to think like them. We need to be intentional with what we are thinking on repeat. When we intentionally choose thoughts that make us feel capable, proud, confident, relaxed, and successful and think them 51% of the time, they become our most dominant thoughts. We are reprogramming the old disempowering thoughts we learned from the past with new empowering thoughts to create our future. Use these if they benefit you, or create your own. But find ones you can read several times a day. The more often you read them and *feel* them, the quicker your new empowered identity will emerge. Remember, the repetition of thoughts and emotions creates new beliefs. Which results in new actions, which lead to new results.

Paradigms are more than just a way of feeling, thinking, or believing. They are a way of BEING! How you are showing up in the world and the actions you are taking.

1. Abundant Leaders are 100% responsible 100% of the time for their actions and results, without guilt or blame.

2. Abundant Leaders understand "Sacred Self" Care is the foundation of sustainable practice and give themselves plenty of space for their non-negotiables.

3. Abundant Leaders look for opportunities and possibilities.

4. Abundant Leaders choose abundance, even when others choose scarcity.

5. Abundant Leaders believe their most dominant thoughts create their results; therefore they take daily action to align to what they most want to receive.

6. Abundant Leaders allow themselves to take risks and course correct.

7. Abundant Leaders commit before they know how.

8. Abundant Leaders do what they need to do with integrity and live authentically.

9. Abundant Leaders make powerful, decisive choices often.

10. Abundant Leaders believe there is no failure, only feedback and learning.

11. Abundant Leaders trust themselves and take inspired action daily.

12. Abundant Leaders are impact-driven and give generously.

Which one of these will you choose to put on repeat today?

Imagine that you believed it 100%. What would be different about your life? Your business? Your relationship with yourself and your relationship with others? Can you see the power of your belief system in creating your success?

Doing this daily is what I call "doing the reps." Just like going to the gym because you want to build strength. It's a practice. It's not a one-and-done. Lifting weights just once in a while will not create a permanent change. It's the same with cultivating a growth mindset. It's ongoing. So, how do you incorporate this into your daily life?

Here are a few ideas I use:

• Audios with affirmations.

• Notes on my desk or around the house with what I want to believe. Such as, "Money flows to me easily and quickly."

• My clients are everywhere.

• This is the perfect time to start and grow a business.

• I have everything I need.

• I am safe.

• I am loved.

• I belong.

• My bank account is growing every day.

• There are so many ways to make money.

• Reading inspirational books.

• Looking for success stories.

• Meditations that lead you through positive affirmations.

• Creating a belief plan to read each morning and night.

• Working with a coach to help you reframe your thoughts.

There are multiple ways to do this easily. The key is to find something that you like. I'll share a few of my favorite resources in the resource section of this book so you can have a place to start.

In this chapter, you learned:

• Course correcting is a critical part of the entrepreneurship journey.

• The Eight Obstacles to Success and multiple ways to overcome them.

• When we know where we bump up against an obstacle and have practical steps to overcome it, we remain empowered in our leadership as CEOs of our businesses and can continue to grow.

• 12 Abundant Leader Paradigms for Success: These ways of BE-ING guide our thoughts and actions as we grow thriving and successful businesses that impact the lives of others.

• Neuroscience is the fast track to taking action and creating success.

• Repetition creates beliefs

Conclusion: You did it!! You've gone through all six steps of the Soulful Abundance System® and I'm celebrating you with a big virtual hug and a toast of bubbly to you. You're now ready to dive in and get to work to start changing lives and creating a prosperous, holistic business. Just remember, some days will feel like you're in the flow and you can't believe how great things are going, and some days it will feel like nothing is working and you're just pushing a giant boulder up a hill with the top nowhere in sight. When things start feeling hard, I want you to remember that No ONE creates success by giving up. Everyone who has created success has had the same crazy days that felt like they were going sideways. But they used that as information. Not a reason or an excuse to give up. You have this passion in your heart for a reason. Which means success is inevitable as long as you keep going. The fact that you are reading this book today is your sign that NOW is your time. By reading this book and implementing these strategies, you are now part of a greater community of empowered women who are here to make a difference in our world. So keep asking questions, reach out for support, get in the rooms with other women who cheer you on and want you to succeed, and know that I am sending high vibes for success your way. Every day, I say a prayer for success to everyone in my world, whether I know them personally or not. So know that you are included just because you are holding this book. I'd love to meet you, be a part of your success journey, and see you inside our virtual community, too. We are a group of heart-centered leaders who lead with love and believe in playing the generosity game, and we'd love to have you with us. Because we are so much stronger collectively than we are on our own. "Together we rise, sister."

You can join us here.

In part two, I'll share with you how to create a cash infusion in your business in 30 days or less. In part one, I shared with you the entire Soulful Abundance System®, which is the complete strategy to build a thriving and sustainable Six-Figure and beyond business. But sometimes, you just need an injection of CASH. Maybe the client inflow is lower than you expected, or you want to invest in something and need some extra income for the month. In that case, you need a short-term strategy for creating cash anytime you need it. This is my gift to you. A bonus for getting this far. I normally only teach this inside my programs with my clients, but I want you to have this, too. So you can feel empowered to create cash anytime you need it and know just what a powerful creator you are.

Part 2
The Short-Term Strategy to Making Money in Your Business

"A strong woman looks a challenge dead in the eye and gives it a wink." — **Gina Carey.**

Create a CASH INFUSION in 30 days or LESS.

In this BONUS chapter, I'll share with you the exact strategy we use inside Activate Abundance® Academy to create $2000 - $10,000 in 30 days or less. It's a skill you must have in building your holistic business in the entrepreneurship landscape today.

Please note- this strategy is a short-term strategy because it is based on your WARM leads in your ecosystem. It is not designed to be used to try and convince new or cold leads to buy. At any time, you have at least 200-300 warm leads in your audience. I'll show you how to identify them, where to find them, and what to offer them so you can serve with your heart and be well compensated for your service.

Let's dive in.

Here are the four steps we will cover.

Christine Williams

1.Setting yourself a really big goal to reach by the end of 30 days (something that will stretch you)

2.Making a plan for how you're going to make it happen

3.Committing to making it happen

4.Taking massive action to reach your goal

STEP 1: Pick your goal

"Setting goals is the first step in turning the invisible into the visible." Tony Robbins

In order to achieve something amazing this month, you need to get clear about what it is you want to achieve.

Instead of focusing on trying to achieve lots of things, pick one big goal to focus on and make it your priority.

When you get laser-focused on achieving one thing, you'll make so much more progress

What one big goal would you like to reach by the end of 30 days?

Get really clear, and don't hold yourself back. Take a moment to journal on what your desire is for income in the next 30 days.

- Why do you want to achieve it?

- How will it make you feel?

- What are you going to do with the money?

- What opportunities will this open for you, your family, and your community when you have this money?

Take a few moments to really connect with this feeling. Then, as you visualize yourself achieving this goal, write down how you feel. This is your home base energy. This is the feeling you want to return to day after day, as it's the feeling of YOU already having it.

EXERCISE

SEE IT, FEEL IT, BELIEVE IT

Throughout this month, I want you to spend at least 10 minutes a day (five minutes in the morning, five minutes in the evening) visualizing achieving your goal.

Step 1:

1. Close your eyes

2. Take a few deep breaths and relax

3. Create a movie in your mind: I want you to imagine that it's the end of the month and you've reached your goal. What

can you see? How do you feel? Vividly imagine it like it's happened – connect with the feeling

Taking time every single day to see your goal being accomplished, to feel it being accomplished, and to believe that you will accomplish it is so powerful.

By focusing on what you want to achieve, you will draw to your people, ideas, and inspiration to help you make it happen.

The cool thing is this is actually backed by science. Your RAS (Reticular Activating System) in your brain does the heavy lifting by filtering out information you don't need and bringing information to you that you do need. **In the book "The Organized Brain," Daniel J Leviton, PhD writes:**

"Millions of neurons are constantly monitoring the environment to select the most important things for us to focus on. These neurons are collectively the attentional filter. They work largely in the background, outside of our conscious awareness. This is why most of the perceptual detritus of our daily lives doesn't register, or why, when you've been driving on the freeway for several hours at a stretch, you don't remember much of the scenery that has whizzed by: Your attentional systems "protects" you from registering it because it isn't important."

So what about all the things that magically appear in our lives to get us to our goals? We start to see signs everywhere that we did not see before. Maybe it is not so much that they appeared, but that they were always present, and we just filter it out until it becomes relevant to us. By focusing on what we

WANT, the RAS gets into action and has us look for the signs that we need to see to support our goals. It really is true, what you focus on GROWS.

So don't skip this step. It's important for you to see the signs and opportunities, people, and ideas that will propel you to accomplish your big-money goal.

Step 2: Make your plan

There are lots of ways to create a cash infusion, but I'm going to give you an example of three that I use.

Choose ONE of these to go all in on for the next 30 days.

1. EASY YES offer priced at around $500.

This gives amazing value at a crazy price. Is easily accessible for your client and provides a specific result.

Some examples that my clients have used for this offer are:

• Package bundles

• Private access to you for 30 days.

• A deep dive assessment

• A course bundle

- One-day workshops

- Group VIP day

- Special pricing on packages plus additional bonuses that are valued at around $1,000.

You want the value of this offer to be at least double what you are charging so that the value stands out.

2. Irresistible offer- Priced around $1,000 and above.

This is a mega value at an irresistible price. Think of this as a next-level opportunity for your clients to work with you in a special container of time. This is not an offer that you normally have publicized, so it's a special and exciting opportunity.

One way this looked for me was to invite a select few clients to work with me privately in a one-month container. I normally only work with clients in six-month or one-year time containers, so this was an opportunity for those who wanted more private support to have that at a fraction of the price. I normally charge $2,500 a month for a month of support, and I offered this irresistible offer for only $1,500 for just five people. It sold out in three days just by making personal invitations to a select few that I really wanted to invite into this. This cash infusion created $7,500 in just three days' time, and my clients were very happy about this opportunity.

3. Exclusive and limited-time offer- $ 2,000 and beyond.

This is one of my favorites. It's a limited-time offer for a certain number of clients or a limited time frame. I like to combine this with the irresistible offer above.

An example of this might look like:

• The next two people who book a VIP day get it at a special price (normally priced at $5,000, they can get it for $3,000) PLUS private access for 30 days and a bonus call two weeks after the month ends for a check-in.

• A VIP upgrade when someone decides to work with you in a group program.

• A special 48-hour savings

• An exclusive offer that you don't offer regularly and is a one-time offer.

The important thing to remember is to create an offer that feels FUN for you. If it's not something you want to deliver on, don't create it. This needs to be an offer that you can get your energy behind and be super excited about and feel jazzed about the value that someone will get when they invest in it. Your energy matters when it comes to making an offer to your potential clients.

If you can't decide on what to offer for your cash infusion, a fun game that I learned from my coach and mentors is to play the "50 ways to make money game That I mentioned earlier.

COMMIT TO MAKING IT HAPPEN

Let's take a few moments to align your energy and raise your financial ceiling to receive this next amount of income.

The body never lies…so if there is physical discomfort in your body when you consider receiving more money than you have ever received before at one time, it is a powerful sign you will energetically repel this level of abundance coming to you in real life.

Think about your goal. How do you feel in your body? What kind of impact are you making with your clients in the world?

Is there anything you need to let go of to step into the empowered version?

Create your daily belief plan. What are 10 empowering beliefs that will allow you to embody this version of you receiving this money?

Some examples are:

• Money is easy to create.

- It's easier to make lots more money than it is to make less.

- People are looking for this offer, and I can't wait to see who decides to say YES.

- Money gives me incredible freedom, possibility, and choice.

- I believe in being wealthy, abundant, and joyful.

- There's plenty of money for everyone.

- The more money I make, the more impact I make on others.

- I LOVE my pricing!

- I could easily double my fees and my clients would happily invest with me.

- I am in the flow of the currency of money and abundance.

It's your turn. Write down 10 empowering beliefs that FEEL good and support the belief that you CAN accomplish this goal.

Step 3: TAKE ACTION

You have decided what your offer will be and who in your ecosystem. You have decided what you want to price it at. Now, it is time to take action and enroll the clients.

Make a love list of 100 people in your WARM market who would be a good fit for this offer.

Some examples of your warm market are:

1. Past clients

2. Current clients

3. Past potential clients who said, "Not yet."

4. Friends that have shown interest in your work and programs

5. People in your Facebook group

6. People on your email list

7. People you have spoken to in a group

8. People you have met at a conference

9. People who have downloaded a free opt-in or lead magnet

10.   People who are in the same programs you are in

11.   Colleagues

12.   Client referrals

13.   People who viewed your Facebook live

14.   People who have come to a challenge, workshop, or masterclass.

Your warm market is anyone who has experience of knowing, liking, and trusting with you.

Once you have made your list, decide how many people you should reach out to personally per day to invite them to hear about your new offer. Remember, out of the total number of people that you reach out to, only 30% of those people will say yes to listening. So make sure you have a good list.

What do you need to do every day for the next 30 days to reach your goal?

Take ACTION. Do something NOW that will help you get closer to achieving your goal. Whether it's sending an email, making a call, or compiling a list, just do something within the next 24 hours. It will help you build momentum.
Reach out to your love list that you created above. I personally like to use the method to reach out that we currently communicate in. If we are messaging each other on Facebook, then I will send them a voice message. If I communicate via email, I'll use email. If I talk to them on the phone, I'll call them.

A sample message that I use goes like this:

"Hi NAME, It's Chris. I just wanted to reach out because I was thinking about you today. I just created something new and wanted to share it with you. I'm not sure if it's a good fit for you or not, so I thought I'd see if this is something you feel would help you with your x,y,z goals. Can I share the details with you?

Short and sweet, easy peasy.

One of the ways to fast-track your success is to track all the ways money and abundance are coming to you. When you write down all of the ways that you are receiving abundance, you change the focus from what you "don't" have to what you DO have. And it all counts.

Four things to track daily:

1. Money that comes to you daily. Refunds, cash, someone paying for lunch or coffee, new clients, upgrades, gifts, new money.

2. For your abundant mindset activities, write down what you do in the morning and what you do in the evening.

3. Abundance signs that you see for yourself or anyone else. When you notice abundance or success in someone else, say, "I am one with that", because you saw it, it means it's available for you too.

4. Opportunities: Abundance is opportunities not yet actioned. Are there people or opportunities that are coming into your awareness that you can take action on?

Tracking these things daily will help you stay focused and intentional about where you are placing your energy. Remember the RAS I mentioned earlier. Tracking helps your brain look for MORE of what you are tracking.

Every spring and fall, I take my clients through this in a live group. Doing this in a community or with a buddy helps you stay inspired and creates the accountability to follow through. Plus, it's so much more fun when everyone is sharing their ideas for a cash infusion, celebrating their wins together, and helping to keep each other encouraged. While I'm writing this, we have just started our spring 2024 Cash Infusion, and our clients are so excited. The creative offers they are sharing have me excited for them. I especially love the offer my client, who is a menopause coach, has decided on. She created a private ½ day VIP day to help her clients recover from the fatigue and anxiety that can happen when going through menopause. She added a bonus of a follow-up call two weeks later and access to a voice messaging app for 30 days. This entire offer was priced at an introductory rate for just five women at $1,497. She made her love list and has already sold three of them just by personally reaching out to women who are in her private Facebook group. She is amazed at how simple and effective this cash infusion process is and how it worked to bring income into her business quickly.

In this chapter, you learned:

- Three specific strategies to create a cash infusion anytime you need it.

- 3 strategies to implement that will help you create cash in your business.

- What to put in your cash infusion offer.

- How to price your offer to be an "easy YES"

In Part 3, you'll hear from past and current clients about how they are using the Soulful Abundance System® to grow thriving, heart-centered holistic businesses that they love.

Part 3
Soulful Abundance Stories

"The question isn't who is going to let me; it's who is going to stop me." — **Ayn Rand.**

I wanted to share a few stories from some of my clients who are doing big work and using the Soulful Abundance System® to build thriving holistic businesses. I'm letting them speak in their own words about how changing the way they approached their business has impacted them in the growth process of their success. On days when you feel like nothing is working, come back to these stories. These are real-life stories shared by real women just like you. They started from scratch and had a dream to serve, help people and have a thriving business that was in alignment with their values. None of these women are unicorns. They don't have access to a secret key to the client closet. They learned, implemented, and kept at it on repeat. Being an entrepreneur is not for the faint of heart. It requires emotional resilience, determination, and belief in possibility. I hold that possibility and vision with you and know you absolutely have what it takes to be successful. You've got this.

"We need to reshape our own perception of how we view ourselves. We have to step up as women and take the lead." — **Beyoncé.**

Amy Willis:

My name is Amy C. Willis. I am the Holistic Sober Coach and the founder of Hol + Well. I have been working professionally as a sober coach since 2019 and work predominantly with women and folks within the LGBTQ+ community who are interested in entering and sustaining sobriety while building lives they don't want to escape from. In addition to being a dual-certified coach, I am also a yoga and meditation teacher and an EFT practitioner.

My work is deeply personal to me as I struggled with a severe addiction to alcohol for many years and also lost my dad to his alcohol addiction. In finding sobriety in 2016, I found myself and reclaimed my freedom and power in the process. Through my coaching work and various offerings, I am deeply committed to supporting as many women and queer folks as possible in finding freedom in sobriety while also shifting how we talk about, think about, and engage with alcohol in an effort to reduce alcohol-related harms.

After many years of struggling with addiction, the turning point and catalyst was my dad's unexpected passing in 2014. My dad's death rocked my world, threw me even further into my addiction, and ultimately served as a turning point for me to look critically at my relationship with alcohol and, subsequently, get sober in 2016.

Getting sober was the single most powerful and empowered decision I have made to date, and through my own experiences in sobriety, I felt inspired and called to support others in their sober journeys. I completed my dual coaching certifications in 2019 and launched my business immediately after. My coaching training provided some business basics but I found that for the first few years of my business, I was mostly throwing spaghetti against the wall to see what stuck. While my business was growing and thriving, the growth (and income) was inconsistent, and I hadn't yet figured out systems and strategies that were both effective, actionable, and sustainable.

I joined Chris's Facebook group for heart-centered entrepreneurs in December 2022 and have been learning from her ever since. One of the best suggestions Chris gave me early on was to start a private community where I could nurture, support, and love sober and curious women. I took Chris's sage advice, and that group is now my favorite corner of the internet as it allows me to show up in service of my community and provide ongoing support and care.

Chris's approach to business and coaching is entirely refreshing; she truly embodies service and generosity, graciously lending her business expertise and savvy to those who are seeking it. I have engaged with Chris in a multitude of ways, including in her Facebook groups, free workshops and masterclasses, in a laser coaching session, and most recently in her Cash Flow Accelerator program, and what I can say with certainty is that working with and learning from Chris has profoundly and positively impacted all areas of my business. By implementing what she has taught me, I have developed clear, focused, and effective strategies and practices, expanded my reach, exposure, and impact, cultivated an engaged community, and ultimately, generated more consistent income along the way. I have also benefited significantly from Chris's coaching around mindset, which has fundamentally changed how I show up in and experience my business. Chris truly embodies and models a heart-centered approach, which shines through in her ongoing investment in her community, her commitment to collaborations, and how she regularly creates opportunities to bolster and amplify others. I am exceedingly grateful to Chris for her wisdom, generosity, and guidance, and I can't wait to continue our work together.

Jennifer Turner-

Hello, my name is Jennifer Turner. I'm a grief recovery and abundance coach. I am the founder of the Facebook Group Abundantly You – Recover Your Light after Loss and the creator of The Grief to Serenity Pathway. My mission is to guide individuals through their own struggles with grief and help them find a path toward healing and abundance.

My personal experience with the loss of my best friend, Jamie, had a significant negative impact on my life and health. When I faced my own health challenges, I decided to tackle them head-on. I wanted to take a holistic approach, dealing with both the physical and emotional sides of my well-being while navigating through grief.

I made it my mission to dig deep into the core issues of grief, not just skimming the surface. Through this process, I found using a mixture of methods like therapy, meditation, journaling, essential oils, and guided meditation really made a difference in my recovery. Now, as a certified guided meditation practitioner, I'm happy to share what I've learned with others who might be going through similar challenges. I obtained my Health Coaching Certification in 2014, but I struggled to find clients and, as a result, continually felt like a failure. After Jamie's passing, it became a significant challenge to guide others towards a healthier life when I struggled to take care of myself.

As part of my journey to "rise from the ashes of grief," I made a promise in Jamie's honor that I would reclaim my role as a health coach. So, it is no coincidence that I met Chris Williams in November of 2022 at a business retreat in Savannah, Georgia. Chris's kindness, genuine love for people, and vibrant energy were immediately apparent.

After the retreat, I started following Chris on Facebook. Less than a year later, I found myself on a call with her to explore the possibility of working together and taking my coaching aspirations to the next level. And has it ever!!

Ever since I began using the Soulful Abundance System®, it's been a game-changer in more ways than I expected, not just for my business but for my personal and professional growth as well. Chris doesn't just throw business strategies at you; she adds this heart-centered, holistic touch that's made a real impact on every part of my life.

One moment that has had a profound impact on my business was during a strategy call with Chris. We were talking about finding ideal clients and uncovering my unique "secret sauce." Chris suggested bringing my personal experience with grief into my coaching. This has truly taken me from failure with no clients to the grief recovery & abundance coach with the perfect ideal client and a program that I am honored and excited to offer. What an a-ha moment!

The real gem of the program for me is the Attract / Nurture / Invite Trio. My coaching school never covered how to pull in clients, nurture those connections, and invite them to work with you. It's been the missing link in my previous coaching programs and has changed how I view and offer my programs.

Following the system has redefined and ignited my coaching business and has been a catalyst for positive change and growth in my life, and it still holds the title for the best decision made.

Shari Biery:

National Board Certified Health & Wellness Coach

Alive With Purpose Health and Life Coaching, LLC

In 2019, I found myself equipped with a new health and life coaching certification, filled with aspirations to start my own wellness practice. However, the path forward was clouded with uncertainty. One evening on Facebook, I stumbled upon Christine Williams, who was conducting a virtual workshop on building a successful wellness business.

Little did I know this encounter would become the key that unlocked the door to my entrepreneurial journey. Before connecting with Chris, my post-certification phase felt like attempting to construct a house without a blueprint. I undervalued my coaching skills and grappled with life's many distractions. With Chris' transformative coaching programs— Launch Well, Activate Abundance, Activate Abundance Alumni, and the Accelerate Mastermind—she emerged as my guiding light. These programs weren't just about business strategies but a holistic approach to personal growth and transformation in a community of other heart-centered women.

Through Chris' coaching, I learned how to attract clients and the importance of consistent connection. Chris showed me how to successfully build a community in an online wellness practice. Weekly Facebook Lives became a staple, creating a space for meaningful interactions within a community that I grew to over 200 members—a testament to the strategic guidance provided through Chris's coaching.

The true magic unfolded in executing three successful launches for my group coaching program, *Nourish With Purpose*. Chris's mentorship turned my dreams into tangible realities. These launches were not merely about selling services but invitations for other women to embark on a transformative journey to a better life with me as their coach.

What sets Chris apart is her unwavering commitment to collaboration. Her programs bring in experts who share specialized knowledge. This collaborative approach became a game-changer, expanding the horizon of my learning journey and providing unique perspectives.

This chapter in my entrepreneurial story is a testament to the impact of Chris's coaching programs. It goes beyond business strategies, encompassing a holistic transformation—from building my confidence as a coach to embracing a consistent self-care plan while building a successful coaching business.

These achievements and collaborative experiences prove the practical impact of Chris and her coaching programs. I'm profoundly grateful to have had Chris helping me in the early stages of my coaching business. The lessons I learned while implementing the Soulful Abundance System have helped me continue building and growing a wellness practice that I love.

Stephanie Pazniokas:

Once upon a time, I was a newly divorced woman with young children and a solid education - having gotten my Master's in Neuroscience before starting a family. I suddenly had to get a job, put my toddlers into daycare, and see all of the dreams and expectations of how my life would happen to get dashed.

I found a job, climbed the ladder, and ended up in a position doing some really cool work. Unfortunately, all of that was at the expense of my health and relationships. I was traveling and eating out a lot, and I had gained somewhere around 50 lbs on my 5'3" frame, developed pre-diabetes (type II diabetes runs strong in my family), high blood pressure, joint pain, jaw pain, back pain, swollen feet, and worst - depression, hopelessness, sleep issues, anxiety and simply zero energy. I "relaxed" with a bottle of wine - and sequestered myself from my family and friends when I was between business trips so I could "recover." I was in my late 30s and felt entirely trapped and hopeless.

(Re)Start the yo-yo diet roller coaster here (I had definitely dabbled with this in my late 20s!). I did an off-the-shelf program that did allow me to lose weight but in a very unhealthy way. I had SOME energy back, and SOME aspects of my health DID look better on paper, but the way that I went about it wasn't sustainable at all. It sort of nerfed my metabolism and made me a hangry, irritable person. High exercise and calorie restriction are not a great combination.

The real kicker was that I was changing so many things at once that my body never really adjusted well…and neither did my mind. The program had a number in it - so I only had to do it for so long…then I could go back to normal, right? Well, normal is 88% of the population of the US being metabolically unhealthy…do I want normal?

In the throws of another high-stress job at a start-up, my mom was diagnosed with terminal lung cancer - and now, while I was managing my physical health (the right way), my stress levels were sky-high, and health issues started creeping back in. My daughter also was having health issues and then became pregnant. As a very young mom-to-be, she needed my help.

Christine Williams

It was time for a career change - a passion that had been growing from the seed of my pain for a long time finally bloomed into something official. All of my scientific training, corporate experience in business, product management, project management, marketing, and sales, as well as my nutritional experience and training, opened up a whole new world.

Starting a health coaching business is no small thing. There is no guarantee of success, and I knew my chances were very small if I didn't get help. I ran across Chris William's coaching practice and the Soulful Abundance System® when she hosted a summit of business coaches, and my world opened up. This new thing I never knew existed. I signed up with a sales coach and then a marketing coach…but I knew ultimately that Chris' Activate Abundance Academy was going to be my landing place. I didn't want to use the traditional sales methods from corporate, and I knew I needed a "full service" business coach. A coach who would help me serve and nurture to my heart's content AND still make money. My first year with Chris 3x'd my income from my first year in business as I learned Chris's Soulful Abundance System® and how to build my community, create a masterclass and other nurture events, and create strategic partnerships and collaborations that are win-win-win services for everyone.

I am looking to do even more this year as I am stretched again and again beyond my "comfort zones" with Chris and the community of Activate Abundance firmly in my corner and I in theirs. As of this writing, I have created more income in the first 4 months of 2024 than in the entire year of 2023. I've had my largest income and clients months yet, and I am putting the Soulful Abundance System® on repeat to create my next level of success.

Margaret Harle:

In the late Spring of 2020, I was in a meeting with my healing group at A Healing Collective. We were meeting to standardize our procedures for infection control and sanitizing our office space. We were in the midst of a world pandemic, and we wanted to keep our clients safe. The very next day, an announcement was made that all non-essential businesses had to close. I was not considered essential, and I had to pause my business.

I am a holistic practitioner, a nurse, an energy therapist, and a Healing Touch practitioner. My business, or practice, as I like to call it, was hands-on, in-person, and high touch. Now, I was unable to see my clients in person. I scrambled around and developed a program I could offer over the phone. I had never used Zoom and wasn't sure what I was doing or if it would work.

A friend told me about Christine Williams and directed me to her Facebook page. She was just starting a masterclass on Facebook, and I tuned in every day. I was so amazed at all the content; it was virtually just what I needed to launch my virtual business. After the class I signed up right away for Activate Abundance Academy to learn the Soulful Abundance System®. I was planning to go to Europe for a vacation, and that was not going to happen because of COVID-19, so I used my vacation money to pay for Activate Abundance Academy.

What I loved about the Soulful Abundance System® was the mindset and the daily alignment. I was an energy worker. After all, I did this stuff all the time for other people. I remember the first week of the program, every day, I just said to myself, "I am worthy. My worth is innate. I was born worthy, I am worthy to have an abundant practice, to support myself to the level I need to have an incredible practice."

The next thing I loved was developing my signature system. I spent weeks tweaking my system until I had it down. My very own signature system that included every aspect of my work. When I had my system down, my confidence level in my practice just skyrocketed. I am a very creative person, and immediately, I had ideas for everything…books, programs, and courses. I felt like I had created a framework for my legacy work. I have been an energy healer for over 30 years, but I needed structure around creating my content, plus accountability and support. Chris provided all of this.

The model of my business prior to working with Chris was 100% self-referral. The thought of inviting people to work with me was new. I was uncomfortable with it. Listening to Chris week after week talking about Attract, Nurture and Invite eased my apprehension. It took practice, but after a while, it became easier.

In working with Chris, I discovered that I had some really unhelpful thoughts about money. Due to my life circumstances and my personality, I was uncomfortable charging what my work was really worth. Within six months of working with Chris, I raised my prices by 40%. It was so scary, but person by person, my new clients paid my price without blinking.

I still have loads of room to grow and expand, and now I have a hybrid practice that is part in-person and part virtual. I am also moving into doing more group programs.

What I will always need is support, refocusing, and inspiration. Something Chris always says is, "We always need support because when we are in the jar, we can't read the label."

Allissa:

My journey to establish Shine Sound Therapy, LLC, like many people's journeys, started with some powerful personal experiences.

I'm a long-time believer in natural medicine and a holistic approach to health and well-being. It's something I practice at my home in De Pere, Wisconsin, with my husband, Adam, two daughters, and even our Cavapoo pup, Stella. A grueling experience when I was tested for Lyme disease reinforced my need to do two things:

1. Be my own advocate.

2. Listen to my gut when I sensed something wasn't quite right.

When I was first diagnosed with Lyme disease, I tried the traditional medications that my doctor recommended. However, I continued to endure symptoms ranging from a numb face and hands to sharp shooting pains. All I could think was, "This isn't normal. I know my body, and I know things aren't right."

This led me to pursue care from a holistic doctor who looked at me as a whole person and used elements of both traditional and alternative medicine to successfully manage my health.

That experience reinforced how important my intuition was, and to heed it.

So, when I sensed I needed to leave my career as a construction project coordinator - to accommodate our busy family lifestyle and to honor my need for a less stressful career - my family was on board with that.

I was listening to my intuition, even though I didn't know where things would go next. I just sensed I was being called to do something more with my life…that I wasn't yet fulfilling part of my purpose.

After leaving my construction career in April 2022, I happily turned my attention to spending a summer with my girls and training Stella. Summer is such a short window here in Wisconsin, and I had visions of all the fun outings and activities we would do. Unfortunately, out of nowhere, I was caught off guard by severe anxiety and panic attacks. When I thought about it, I realized they could have been triggered by leaving my job. I did feel like I had lost a piece of identity, even though I knew I was doing the right thing. The panic attacks and anxiety reared up, and they tied my stomach up in knots, and worry overshadowed every other aspect of my life.

I was able to function - but barely. This wasn't living! It existed, and always with worry about when the next episode would strike. I knew I needed to do something. I didn't want to take anti-anxiety prescription medication, but at the same time, I wasn't sure where to turn. That's when a conversation with my aunt reminded me of how my uncle had successfully used sound therapy to conquer an addiction.

And after doing some praying, reading, and deliberating, I thought, "What is the harm in trying it?" If it didn't work, I could always go back to the chalkboard.

I scheduled my first session in June 2022. Imagine my surprise when I sensed a change, a fundamental shift, *that same day*. It was like the sound practitioners dissolved some of the emotions causing my panic attacks. I still felt some of those emotions, but it was like I could look at them with some emotional distance.

As days went by, there were things that would come up that used to make me sick to my stomach, at best, or cause a panic attack, at worst. But after the sound therapy, I was able to handle those situations. There was a sense of calm and peace I felt that wasn't there before.

Fast forward several months to today, and I haven't had a panic attack since. Anxiety or worry might creep up on occasion, but I am able to just observe those thoughts and feelings rather than having them run rampant through my body. I've been able to live my life without anxiety limiting my abilities.

Sound therapy got to the root of my issues.

By August 2022, I knew I wanted to help others experience the life-changing benefits of sound therapy. I sensed there was divine intervention leading me to the next chapter of my career. More than that, I sensed I was answering a calling in my heart. Where else would I have the opportunity to combine my intuitive nature, compassion, sensitivity, caring personality, and passion other than in a career in sound therapy?

I felt a sense of peace and alignment when I made the decision.

I obtained my sound therapy certification from Rediscover Yourself soon after and then followed my intuition in naming my business Shine Sound Therapy, LLC. My business name feels right because it is aligned with the message shared in Matthew 5:16:

"Let your light shine before others, that they may see your good deeds and glorify your Father in heaven."

For me, the details of getting a business up and running were very strategic and I was focused on each detail. My years of construction planning and scheduling were still being put to good use. I had my logo, website, business cards, and paperwork all complete and was ready to open the doors to my business. These details were great, but I felt there was something missing.

I had begun to see clients in my new space, and word was slowly getting out there about my new business. People were excited and supportive, but the appointments were few and far between. My confidence was slowly sinking as all my hard work and excitement did not match the number of people I was hoping to help.

One day, I was online and some information for Chris's Soulful Abundance System® appeared. She was leading a free three-day program to help simplify your business and do it soulfully. My initial thought was this aligned with my business and beliefs, but I wanted to be sure, so I attended the event and immediately resonated with what Chris was discussing. I was very comfortable with her and felt good about her ideas.

Within a few weeks, we had our first clarity call where she answered all of my questions and provided me with the support I needed to assist me in making the best decision for my business and my family. After talking with my husband, we knew Chris's Activate Abundance Academy program was a good fit for me.

The Activate Abundance® Academy program and Chris have helped me think outside of the box and take off my blinders when looking at my business. I was so wrapped up in the details and having everything so perfect that I was missing the opportunities right in front of me. Working through the

Soulful Abundance System's Invite step helped me to feel more confident when speaking about my offers. The Invite step helped me find clarity around the ways I could help women and how to invite them to work with me in a way that felt in service to them and in alignment with my values. Since joining Active Abundance Academy I have also added singing bowls to my offerings in order to be able to share the gift of sound healing with groups and not just one-on-one. I have also connected with so many other women entrepreneurs who know and understand the challenges of being a wellness coach or practitioner.

The Soulful Abundance System® has been a game changer in my business. Having simple steps to focus on and implement on repeat, along with the customized support, was exactly what I needed. The process works. You can read 100s of books and watch videos all day long, but in the long run, we all need the right system, support, and community to be accountable and create movement within ourselves and our business.

Vikki:

I am the owner of The Bodyology Clinic, LLC, where women come to build rapport with their intuition and integrate messages from body, mind, and spirit. They learn to do this with Somatic skills, which tap into their highest potential for utilizing their full power—thus claiming their feminine authority.

I opened my clinical practice after recovering from my own personal injury in a car accident that resulted in years of chronic neck and back pain. Before learning therapeutic bodywork modalities, I had been relying on ineffective traditional Western medicine treatments. Over 25 years ago, when I first discovered healing in therapeutic bodywork, it was considered a non-traditional healing modality, yet I experienced miraculous outcomes in these techniques. I instantly found a home in the belief in the body's capabilities to heal itself.

As a young 20-something-year-old, I dove deep into helping others heal from chronic pain to find relief, similar to what I had experienced with bodywork. More than a decade into my private practice, I was hit with another big wound, but that of the heart and mind. My first marriage fell apart, and I became a single mom overnight. With two very small boys to raise, I was dealt a very difficult hand. This healing required matters of habit change in my mind and challenged my belief system about what I thought would be possible for not only me but also my kids. To fully have the life I wanted required me to take a giant leap of faith, put my head down, focus on my vision, and follow through like I'd never done before. Doing so required new lifestyle habits. This experience forced me out on another healing quest that helped me further untangle the relationship between the mind and spirit while examining the limits of my body.

Our brain doesn't differentiate between physical and emotional pain. The trouble is when things aren't going well. We often question our self-esteem and personal power. During this difficult time, I stopped believing my intuition, and my confidence was shaken to my core.

I thought because I had made mistakes and misjudged circumstances in my life, that my intuitive system was faulty, and couldn't be trusted. That's what most people get wrong. Just because bad things happen or you make mistakes doesn't mean your intuition failed you and you can't trust yourself.

What I actually learned during that time was intuition doesn't go away when life is difficult, or we make mistakes. In fact, when things get hard, that's the time we most want to be able to tap into and trust our intuition. Building intuition and self-esteem are an essential part of our healing process and are how we move past healing and start enjoying the life we were given. Our intuition and self-esteem help us make the very best of ourselves during the time we have here!

After all, I had been through, what I noticed most was that navigating through all the hard stuff I had been through was actually quite essential in my journey to reconnect with my intuition, build self-confidence, and deepen my self-esteem. Discovering how to overcome struggles myself inspired me to help others overcome their own personalized stress-pain loops and to teach a more active approach to moving past wellness obstacles. Now, I know no matter what I face, I can handle it. When I met Christine, she helped me embody this even more deeply.

Christine added a practical business perspective to the ways I wanted to serve my clients. What plagued the practical side of my business was having three separate modalities: body, mind, and spirit and I couldn't understand how to weave them together into an integrated offer in a way that made sense to my clients. Doing it alone wasn't working. I needed support to get to the other side.

When I met Chris, I immediately connected with her journey and success as a mother and wellness entrepreneur. I felt like she understood what I had overcome and my struggles of building a wellness practice while juggling the needs of family life. I knew I could build my business, but I doubted I could marry body-mind-spirit modalities into a simple offering without sacrificing time with my family.

I had many coaches before Chris who encouraged me to keep the modalities separate. My spirit just didn't want to believe them, and then Chris came along and held my vision as much as possible. I slowly built hope and trust that what I had to offer was valuable and needed. What I needed was a system to hold the modalities together, a system I could put on repeat that was simple enough that I could manage with my growing family.

Chris's Soulful Abundance System® helped me find my unique advantage and stand out in a saturated market of wellness coaches so that I could talk about my work naturally. In my head, I could see what I wanted but couldn't understand how to pull all that knowledge into a tangible product that would resonate with my clients. With the Soulful Abundance System, Christine helped make it easy to talk about my soul clients, and the process simply came down to attracting, nurturing, and inviting. I now have a clear list of actions that keep my business thriving, I generate consistent income, all while working fewer hours, and having more time with family!

Chris' system is adaptable for working with clients in-person, or virtually. It was adaptable to building my clients through social media or collaborating with local providers because the system remains the same. Simply build your business on a solid foundation, build your audience, and nurture them. She helped me build that basic foundation and know who I'm talking to, what I'm sharing, and how to continue nurturing my audience. Continually connecting and engaging with more people and sharing the work I love makes invitations a very simple task. It's easy to fill my one-on-one slots. I often have a waiting list of clients, and now work a schedule that's seamless with my family's.

As my business continues to grow, the Soulful Abundance System® helped me develop a repeatable system that's still at the heart of my practice. Those steps never change. I'm really grateful for my time with Christine and her holding the potential for my vision to become a reality, and I'm thrilled she makes this powerful system accessible to so many others.

I hope these real-life examples gave you some inspiration. I know it always helps me to see practical ways women grow their businesses. When we see other women succeed, it helps us to believe in our dreams and see that growing a thriving and successful business really is possible. I'd love to share this one last quote with you.

"When the whole world is silent, even one voice becomes powerful." — **Malala Yousafzai.**

Your voice matters. The work you are doing matters. There are people who are looking for you today. They need your services, your support, and your love to guide them from pain island to pleasure island. So SHINE your light, sister! Lead with Love and make the change you were put on this earth to make. It's time to press GO. I'm always cheering you on.

To your ultimate Abundance,

Chris

An Invitation to You

Chris works with clients nationally and internationally in a variety of capacities as a coach, speaker, and consultant.

Chris's core focus areas are:

● How to design, launch, and build your Six-Figure holistic business foundations

● Scaling beyond six figures and breaking the $100,000 ceiling.

● Rapid and sustainable growth strategies using the Soulful Abundance System®

● Heart-centered marketing and Soulful Sales practices that feel good

● Collaborations and strategic partnerships to leverage your time, audiences, and growth.

You can email Chris directly at info@shineabundancenow.com and visit ShineAbundanceNow.com https://shineabundancenow.com/to learn all about Chris's programs, courses, and services.

Christine Williams

To join Chris's exclusive email communities and be the first to receive her training, resources, videos, and more, visit https://shineabundancenow.com

You can also access free trainings on her YouTube channel: Soulful Abundance® with Chris Williams https://www.youtube.com/channel/UCkREo69sxas8TG3gkda _-7g where you can find popular trainings on:

- Where to find paying clients in any economy clients YouTube training

- Unlocking Six-Figure success

- And more

Don't forget to download your free guide: **Business Basics Checklist For Consistent Clients and $10,000 - $30,000 Months here: https://chriswilliams.kartra.com/page/BizBasics**

Acknowledgments

I have been blessed with many people coming in and out of my life for various reasons and seasons who have impacted, inspired, and encouraged me in profound ways. While I can't even begin to mention them all, there are a few I would like to add a special thanks.

First, my Grandma Paula Heath. She started me on the road to women's rights and equality, and without her guidance and love to believe that I could do anything because I Am a powerful woman, I wouldn't be on this mission. From marching with her in the ERA parades in Washington DC to watching her work with grassroots organizations, such as NOW, to help ratify the Equal Rights Amendment and write a calendar with each day of the year dedicated to a woman, I am forever in awe of her dedication and support to help more women come together and be a stand for what is our birthright of opportunities and possibilities. Thank you, Grandma, for encouraging me to be a leader, to play sports instead of being the cheerleader on the sideline, to be inclusive of all people, and to know the importance of paving the way for others and with others.

To my mom for encouraging my independence and going after whatever my dreams were. She is a constant source of love and taught me the value of standing up for what I wanted even when they said, "Girls Can't Play Soccer" when there was only a boys' soccer team. Thank you for standing up to the patriarchy and fighting for me. Thank you for always being there for me in the good times and the struggles. And thank you for cheering me on.

My stepfather, Bob, for encouraging my entrepreneurship, supporting me with your business advice and surrounding us all with love and leadership. You have always treated me as your own daughter and have been one of the best examples of a smart, patient, and kind leader in business and life.

To my Dad for teaching me how to be financially independent and taking ownership of all that I am capable of. From changing the tires on a car to making a budget so I could understand what was needed to support myself to setting up my first LLC, thank you for your love and guidance.

To my husband, Casey, for his never-ending support and encouragement to dream bigger and showing me the power of having a partner who believes in feminine power and not shrinking from my big dreams. I love you.

To my boys, Eli, Ben, and Gabe- You are my lights and loves. Thank you for always believing in your momma, even during the tough times. You inspire me endlessly with your kindness, wisdom, and passion to make this world a better place. You are enlightened young men and I'm so proud of you and blessed to be your mom.

To my coaches who believed in me when I doubted myself and showed me what a powerful feminine business leader looks like and the way to build a soulful business that changed the trajectory of my life. Kaela, Megan, Sara, Liz, Laura, Kendall, Kelly and Kate. I am so blessed by your brilliance in each of your zones of genius. Thank you for paving the way for me and guiding me along this path of entrepreneurship.

To the community of women, I have been blessed to be in rooms with and grow my business within masterminds, events, and retreats. You inspire me and keep reminding me of the powerful work we are all here to do and that our voices matter. Thank you for playing the generosity game with me as collaboration partners, friends and team. Together, we Rise, sisters.

And finally, to my clients. I can not even begin to express my gratitude for allowing me to be on the journey of entrepreneurship with you. It is my honor to be able to serve you, cheer you on, and be your guide as you build your business your way, achieve your dreams, and create a model for the next generation of women watching us. Your courage and dedication to your craft create ripple effects that make our world a happier, healthier place to live. It truly is my honor to support you.

Endnotes and Resources

"Selected portions of these materials for (creating your pricing, signature system, and branding with archetypes) have been legally licensed from the copyright owner, Heart of Success, Inc. Copyright 2024 Heart of Success, Inc."

1.https://writersblocklive.com/blog/women-entrepreneurs-statistics/

2.“Ebook Secrets Exposed” www.EbookSecretsExposed.com:

3.PEW Foundation- https://www.pewtrusts.org/en/

4.“The Organized Mind,” Daniel J Leviton, PhD https://www.penguinrandomhouse.com/books/313653/the-organized-mind-by-daniel-j-levitin/

5.The Thought Model adapted from Brooke Castillo's self-coaching model. https://thelifecoachschool.com/self-coaching-model-guide/

Favorite Books

- A Happy Pocket Full of Money- Gikandi-

- Feeling Is The Secret- Neville Goddard

- The Power of Awareness- Neville Goddard

- Rewired For Wealth- Barbara Stanny

- Sacred Success for Women- Barbara Stanny

- The Science of Getting Rich For Women - Sara Connell

- Who Not How- Dan Sullivan

- The Live Launch Method- Kelly Roach

- The Game of Life - Florence Shinn

- Positive Intelligence- Shirad Chamine

- You Can Heal Your Life- Lousie Hay

YOUTUBE VIDEOS/ CHANNELS

- Brian Scott- Money comes to me easily affirmation

- Mind Valley

- Joe Dispenza

- Bob Proctor

- The White Space Workshop- Christine Williams

- Where To Find Paying Clients In Any Economy- Christine Williams

- Women Thrive Media

Podcasts

- Soulful Abundance With Chris Williams

- RISE - Sara Connell

- The Kelly Roach Show

- EmpowerHER

- Kendall SummerHawk

- Women In Business

About the Author

Christine Williams (Chris) is a sought-after mentor, coach, author, and industry leader on a mission to redefine success for women entrepreneurs—on their terms. Since 2017, she's helped thousands of women start, grow, lead and scale businesses that create real impact —ditching hustle for aligned, soulful and exponential growth. Her innovative, values-driven approach has helped thousands of women break free from both the internal and external limits + outdated models of success so they can build thriving 6 figure and multiple 6-figure sustainable businesses that don't just make money—they change lives, with confidence, freedom and purpose.

Chris challenges the outdated rules of business, empowering women to lead with heart. She helps them transform their expertise into wealth, influence, and a lasting legacy that ripples change into our world—without trading their well-being, values, or integrity for success. Whether it's more time with family, global impact, or the freedom to create limitless opportunities, she helps women build businesses that truly support the life they desire.

A multi-6-figure entrepreneur who built multiple thriving businesses from scratch, Chris doesn't just teach business—she's lived it. More than just building wealth, she's proving that success can be expansive, fulfilling, and aligned. She's igniting a movement of women rising together, rewriting the rules, and owning their power—without sacrificing what matters most.

If you're ready to step into your next level, claim your space, and build a business that not only fuels your life but also transforms the lives of others—Chris is the mentor to get you there. As the author of *The Soulful Abundance System: A 6-Step Guide to Growing a 6-Figure Holistic Business with Purpose*, she provides a proven roadmap for women ready to create wealth, impact, and freedom—without sacrificing their well-being or values.